Confessions of a Female Tour Manager:

This Woman's Life on the Road with Some of the Most Notorious

Rock Bands EVER

by

Kim

(Parkinson Howse Stewart)

Hawes

Introduction

Special Thanks

Introduction

I'll start with a question that's occurred to me more than once in my life: how did a woman who can't play an instrument, sing or read a note of music, who came from a family of non-musicians and who was never all that struck on heavy metal, come to spend ten years of her life sleeping under Lemmy?

There is an answer, intelligible if not very straightforward, and it will emerge in the course of these recollections. (Goodness knows, there was plenty to remember—and thanks to my renunciation of alcohol and drugs, I have.) One thing I can tell you now: as a teenaged punk living in rural Lancashire, I had no idea my life would take the course that it has. It's only now, looking back, that I can make out the shape of it—a life on the road with some of the biggest names in rock 'n' roll history. It's been a pleasure and a privilege, though it didn't always feel that way, and if you'd care to join me, I'd like to tell you all about it.

*

Unmusical as I was, I used to go to a lot of gigs with friends and I never had any trouble getting backstage and meeting bands. The village I grew up in was called Hesketh Bank. It had sprung up as a farming village and by the early 1970s was becoming popular with commuters. Apart from the local youth club, there was nothing for us teenagers to do, so we used to go to concerts.

The first gig I ever went to was David Bowie playing Preston Guild Hall. A neighbour took me and a few friends. After the show, as we were walking back to the car, our ears ringing, we found ourselves in the private parking area. David Bowie's limousine was there waiting, and there, having just emerged from a stage door, was David Bowie making his way over to it. I said hello. He said hello too. Then he got in his car and was driven away. I never imagined that one day I'd meet him again and that it would be Lemmy making the introductions. (At that time I'd never even heard of Lemmy.)

Once I was seventeen and able to drive, we used to go and see bands play at Lancaster University. We saw The Jam there. The hall was rammed and we couldn't get near the stage. Not being tall, we couldn't even see it. We were sat on the floor thinking what a waste of an evening and had decided to leave when one of the crew, seeing us looking dejected and heading for the doors, asked if we'd like to meet the band. Sure, we said. We hung around and after the show we were taken backstage.

It never occurred to me at the time that the guy who made the offer might have had an
ulterior motive for taking two young girls to meet the band. Nothing happened to me though, on this or other, similar occasions.

I should probably here clarify that not only did I sleep under Lemmy, I slept under all of the guys in Motörhead, along with I don't know how many other rock stars (male and female). And when I say I slept under them, I mean I slept on the bunk bed of a tour bus beneath theirs. I always chose the bottom bunk because you could crawl into it. The only disadvantage was the odour of the footwear left just a few feet from my head, which I would combat by spraying the curtain with perfume so that whenever it wafted as someone walked past I'd get a whiff of Chanel No. 5 rather than a smelly shoe size 11.

There were two main factors which set me on a path to spend the greatest part of my life touring with some of the biggest and most notorious bands in music history.

Luck was one of them.

The other was wanting more from life than what seemed to be my lot as a girl growing up in the north of England—a life as a secretary or a shop assistant. Not that I thought there was anything wrong with either of these careers; I just knew they weren't for me.

When an opportunity came my way to go touring with a band—something I had never considered, let alone hoped for—I saw a chance to break out from low middle-class provincial life and to live a life outside the ordinary, to see the world, to have a good time, to escape.

I wouldn't have had the career I've had if I'd let fear get the better of me. There were plenty of times it almost did. That crucial first invitation to go on tour with a band, I almost turned it down. My first proper job as a merchandiser, I almost turned that down too. What stopped me, both times, was the fear that I'd be missing out, that if I didn't take the chance I'd always wonder what might have been, and I knew there wasn't anything I feared so much as that.

When I became a tour manager for a rock band, there wasn't another woman in the world doing what I was doing. Being called Kim, it was almost invariably presumed by those who didn't know me that I would be male and probably bald and burly—that I would, in fact, be pretty much the complete opposite of what I actually was.

I don't pretend that it was all down to me, and in these pages I gratefully acknowledge the many people who helped me get where I did. But I'm not so diffident as to make out that grit and graft and refusal to conform to expectations didn't have a lot to do with it. I was a woman in a man's world, and I wasn't going to give up being a woman. I wouldn't even *try* to be one of the boys. I would be the woman I wanted to be. In thirty years of working with some of rock 'n' roll's brashest and brightest stars, I never ran, never shouted, never gave in and never gave up.

Though we are closer to equality than when I started out, we are not there yet. I hope this book, as well as providing a privileged and entertaining insight into the madcap day-to-day of life on the road, will be an encouragement to women to not surrender their ambitions in the face of the obstacles which remain in this still unequal world, to do what they want to do and to be who they want to be.

There's no reason not to, and it's so much more fun.

1

Getting Out

Of the *Attractions*, the backing band for Elvis Costello, the greatest for me was the keyboardist Steve Nieve. It was a joke with my friend Jackie. Well actually, it wasn't—we were too young for realism to make it one—that one day the two of us would be married, while she would marry Elvis Costello.

It was Wednesday 17th January 1979 and we were in Preston to see the band play the Guild Hall as part of the UK leg of a tour extending across North America, Europe, Japan and Australia. Before the show, over a couple of rum and blacks at the Stanley Arms, Jackie and I made a bet to see who would be able to wangle their way backstage and meet the band. I never got my winnings. In fact, at the end of the night, when I met her at the bus station to catch the last bus to Hesketh Bank, I'd clean forgotten about them. Though I went home with little hope for my marriage to Steve Nieve, I would be seeing him play again with the band. And soon after that, I would be joining them on tour.

*

It was the week before Christmas 1977 and I was staying with a family in Ohio on a school exchange. I was seventeen years old. The father of the family was a doctor working for NASA. I had watched the Apollo 11 moon landing on television almost a decade before and it had made a significant impression on me. I had a sense of being alive at a time when things were happening, and I didn't want to miss out. Sat across the dinner table from this man who was a part of that other world, I had a sense of the nearness of opportunity, that not only was a life working a shop job (as recommended by my educational psychiatrist) something I had *no* interest in whatsoever, but that there really were other lives I might lead.

Later that evening, Elvis Costello was due to make his first appearance on Saturday Night Live after the Sex Pistols, who were originally scheduled to perform, had been waylaid by visa troubles. My exchange family being aware of my punk tastes and my liking for Elvis Costello, we gathered round the television to watch the show. A few seconds into 'Less than Zero', Costello turned away from the microphone and waved his arms at the band saying 'Stop! Stop!' The band stopped. Turning back to the camera, he said, 'I'm sorry ladies and gentlemen, there's no reason to do this song here,' and told the band to play 'Radio, Radio'. They did, and were banned from the show as a result. At the time, failing to register the provocativeness of the stunt—a swipe at corporate control of rock 'n' roll consumption—I was unaware that I had witnessed a moment of music television history.

At the end of my exchange period, I returned to Hesketh Bank and finished at school. I did a modelling course but at five-foot-five I was told I was too short to pursue a career as a model. I was working three days a week on my grandparents' stalls in Blackburn market. My grandmother sold handbags and luggage, my grandfather was a market gardener. I was also training as a swimming instructor at Edge Hill College (now Edge Hill University) in Ormskirk.

Meantime, I was waiting for something to happen.

When Jackie and I heard about Elvis Costello and the Attractions coming to Preston to play the Guild Hall, we didn't hesitate to buy tickets. And so, that Wednesday evening, tasting rum and blackcurrant, we left the stuffy warmth of the smoke-filled pub and briskly walked the short way to the Hall, queued with the other red-cheeked fans, showed our tickets and went through to the auditorium. With money at stake, we decided not to waste the time before the start of the show. We were both quite confident, Jackie perhaps more so than I. We had seen other bands in the past (The Stranglers, The Jam, Ian Dury, the Boomtown Rats, Siouxsie and the Banshees) and had got to know the DJ Andy Dunkley who toured with a number of rock 'n' roll and punk bands. If we could meet Paul Weller without the barest effort, think what we might achieve with a little contrivance. We hitched up our Firoucci jeans and split.

Walking round to the side of the stage, I approached the man who was guarding a door, somewhere behind which the band would be preparing for the show. 'Can I help you?' he said, sounding doubtful. 'I hope so,' I said. 'I was with the band when they did Saturday Night Live in New York.' The man's eyebrows went up. 'You were?' 'Mm-hm,' I nodded, hoping my face wouldn't betray that this was, for all the communion of television, a complete and utter lie. 'Come back after the show,' he said. My heart did a little dance. 'Sure,' I said. 'Thanks very much.' I went off and found my seat. I asked Jackie if she'd got anywhere. She shook her head. Me? Not yet, I told her.

Despite being giddy with anticipation, I remember the show, John Cooper Clarke stalking the stage, Richard Hell and the Voidoids playing a livening set before Elvis Costello and the Attractions finally appeared. Despite the criticism they had received for some lacklustre
performances and a punishing tour schedule, they played a great gig. No sign of fatigue or false feeling.

When the show had finished, I told Jackie I'd meet her at the bus station, and made my way over to the side of the stage, looking for the man I had spoken to earlier. Not seeing him, I hung around the stage door, hoping someone would appear. I'd been stood there a while when the door opened and a man (late twenties, early thirties maybe and bearded) stepped out. Seeing me, he beckoned me over. 'Come with me,' he said. 'I've told them you're here.' I followed him through the door and down a corridor.

'I'm Mike,' he said. Mike Stuart, his name was. He was a promoter's agent for Straight Music, a company run by John Curd, whom I was fortunate to have as a mentor when I entered the touring business later in life. 'Enjoy the show?' he said. Struggling to keep up with him, I said I had, very much. 'You're from Preston?' Not far from, I said, doubting he'd have heard of Hesketh Bank. 'Long way from New York,' he said. I laughed.

When we got backstage, Mike was told that the band had left for the hotel near the bus

station which is now a Holiday Inn. Mike asked if I would like to go over for a drink. My heart did another dance and, nonchalantly as I could, I said, 'Sure.' I looked at my watch and saw that I had about half-an-hour before I had to catch my bus. We went over to the hotel. Mike said they would be in the bar. We walked through the lobby, up a flight of steps and there they were, sat round a table, nursing drinks. I followed Mike to the table and we sat. There was Elvis Costello, Bruce Thomas, the bassist, Pete Thomas, the drummer.

And *there* was Steve Nieve.

'Hello,' he said.

'Hello,' I said. I'm not sure the word quite came out.

A silence ensued. Mike looked between them and me, evidently expecting a flurry of reacquaintance. There was no chance of my saying anything more. Mike shifted in his seat. When it was clear that not a flicker of recognition had passed across the faces of any of the band, Mike said, 'Excuse us a minute,' and signalled for me to follow him. We left the bar.

'So you know the band from Saturday Night Live?'

Not knowing what to say for myself, I said nothing.

'Because I'd say, judging from their reaction just now, either they're collectively amnesiac or that was a fucking porky. Since I've no other reason to suspect the first, I'll say the second.'

I waited to see what he would do. To my surprise, he laughed.

'That's the first time anyone's got one over on me,' he said.

I smiled, relieved. I told him that I *had* seen the Saturday Night Live performance, only not in the studio but in a living room in Ohio. He asked me would I like to stay the night at the hotel. Being naive, it was only later that I understood this to mean, would I like to stay the night *with him*? No thanks, I said; I had to get the bus home. Before I left, he took my phone number and said he would get me a backstage pass to the Oldham gig the following Tuesday. I

thanked him and

apologised for my deception. We said goodbye and I left.

*

I went to the Oldham gig, where I received the pass Mike had

promised, and which I

flaunted when I got home. I hadn't realised that Mike had expected

to see me after the show. The next day I got a phone call from him.

He asked if I would like to join the Elvis Costello tour for the last

few gigs. Would I? Of course. Absolutely. Yes. He said he would

call the following day. I told my mum, who worked as a maths

teacher at the local high school. Though I wouldn't have said so at

the time, she had a much better idea than I did what I—a girl, not a

woman, unworldly-wise—would be letting myself in for were I to

join the tour. She knew, though, what I wanted, and that if she said

no, she would have found my bedroom empty one morning, the

curtains blowing, the window open. Before she said yes, however,

she asked to speak to Mike when he called and asked him for the names, addresses and telephone numbers of all the hotels we would be stopping at. She then called each of the hotels and booked me my own room, so that when I arrived each night I wouldn't find myself having to share with anyone, including Mike—a possibility which, again, being naive, hadn't occurred to me but which had thankfully occurred to my mum.

*

At Preston railway station I bought a single ticket to Bristol. I don't remember being afraid. The purpose of fear is to influence your decisions, and my mind was already made up; there was no chance I was going to change it. I'm sure my thoughts extended only as far as the rest of the tour—less than a week. I didn't know where, if anything, it might lead. I certainly didn't imagine it would lead where it did. All I knew is: I was going on tour with Elvis Costello and the Attractions. How many girls my age could say that?

It was about half-eight in the evening when the train pulled in to Bristol Temple Meads. I found my way to the hotel, checked in, took my bags up to my room and went down to the bar. Mike was there. He told me it had been a day off for the band. He asked how the journey down had been. Fine, I said, and thanked him again for inviting me to join the tour. We had a couple of drinks, then Mike said, 'Come on, better get to bed.' Bed? It was a bit early, I thought. I was buzzing with excitement and alcohol. I finished my drink and followed him to the lift anyway. We got in and he pressed a button. I pressed another.

'What are you doing?' he said.

'I'm going to my room. I'm going to bed.'

'What do you mean, your room?'

'I've booked my own room. I'll see you at the venue tomorrow.'

I got off on my floor and went to my room. Having been granted the privilege of joining the tour, I was determined I wouldn't be a nuisance and was pleased to have shown that I wouldn't need any mothering. I still hadn't realised that Mike's intentions would hardly be described as motherly.

The next morning I found the venue, the Locarno Ballroom (part of the Mecca entertainment complex called the New Bristol Centre on Frogmore Street, since converted into student accommodation). For some reason, Mike wasn't speaking to me. I didn't know why. Nobody else was speaking to me either. It occurred to me then that nobody else knew what I was doing there. Neither, I realised, did I. How was I going to occupy myself over the coming days? I sat down on a flight case and watched the crew unpacking equipment, setting the stage, testing levels. I decided I'd go for a walk. I wandered around the venue, ventured outside, and returned about half-past-five, by which time people were bustling about, hurrying to get everything ready before the doors opened. Someone asked me if I'd seen Lorraine. I said I hadn't. I had no idea who Lorraine was. It was evident from the snatches of conversation I overheard that she was the cause of some concern. I heard someone say she'd been poisoned. Poisoned? I looked around, appalled at the thought of a poisoner in our midst. Had someone called an ambulance? Would she live?

She was most certainly alive when she whirled into the foyer a short while later, clutching her arm and expressing in no uncertain terms that she was in no state to sell T-shirts, just look at her fucking arm. Looking over, I saw the veins in her arm had turned a distinctly blackish hue. 'Christ,' someone said, 'get her to the hospital.' 'What happened?' I asked a fraught-looking man who was shaking his head. 'God knows,' he said. Then: 'Can you sell T-shirts?' I supposed so, having sold bags and flowers with my grandparents on Blackburn market. 'You can sell T-shirts,' he told me. He took me over to the merchandise stall, showed me the stock and told me how to keep the money. And so that night, and on the following nights in Southampton and London, I sold T-shirts for the band. The tour finished. I thanked Mike, said goodbye and went home.

*

It had been a brief but unforgettable experience. I continued working three days a week on my grandparents' stalls and resumed my training as a swimming instructor at Edge Hill. Mike and I had decided to keep in touch, though we weren't in a relationship. After the interruption to normalcy, life would continue as before—at least for the time being. I had no idea how short a time this would be.

I was at home when the phone rang. I answered it and the woman at the other end introduced herself as Eve Carr. She told me she owned the merchandising company I had been working for. She asked if I enjoyed selling T-shirts and said she'd heard I'd been pretty good at it. I told her I did and took the compliment—not imagining that she was coming round to asking me whether I would like to go on another tour. Overcoming my surprise, I said yes, guessing that she meant with Elvis Costello. She didn't. It would be with a band called Rush—six weeks, across Europe.

'Wow,' I said. 'Yes.'

I would be paid, she told me. I didn't ask how much as it wouldn't have made any

difference. I was being offered the chance to go on tour across Europe with a band—never mind I didn't know who they were. (Progressive rock wasn't my thing.) Eve whisked me through the itinerary.Gigs in all the major cities in the UK, then on to Paris, Belgium, Sweden, Norway,

Germany and Switzerland, culminating at the Pink Pop Festival in Geleen, Holland, where Rush would be performing as part of a line-up including The Police, Peter Tosh, Dire Straits, Average White Band, Massada and Elvis Costello. Could I be in London on a certain day? I said I could, and only afterwards looked at the calendar. There was no *way* I wouldn't be.

*

Joining the Elvis Costello tour had meant spending a few days away from home in the south of England. Joining the Rush tour meant I would be spending six weeks away from home all over England and all over Europe too. I hadn't had any misgivings about the first, as I said; the second was something else entirely. It wasn't only the being away from home: it was going away with a band I knew nothing about to places I had only the vaguest notion of—if I'd heard of them at all. There was no Google to find out who Rush was, no Google Earth to make a virtual reconnaissance. A friend's brother played me *Hemispheres*, the band's sixth album which had been released the year before. As I listened to the bizarrely-titled first track, I looked bemusedly at the album cover: a naked male ballet dancer stood on a brain pointing at the Minister of Silly Walks. I opened out the album booklet and looked at the portraits of the band members—Alex Lifeson, Neil Peart, Geddy Lee (who looked to be wearing a sort of kimono)—and wondered what I had let myself in for. I could hear that they were good, excellent musicians, but I wasn't struck on what I heard. After ten minutes or so I asked, 'How long is this song?' 'This is the fourth part,' said my friend's brother. I wondered whether Geddy Lee's voice would last the tour.

The day came for me to take the train to London. That night I would be staying with Lorraine the T-shirt seller, recovered from her pin-badge poisoning. My friends went with me to the station to give me a send-off and I will always be grateful to them that they did. We had some time to kill before my train was due to leave and, on a whim, we decided we'd go to watch the dog-racing. For the hour or so we spent watching the dogs tearing round the track, I wasn't thinking about my impending departure, which was just what I needed.

When I got on the train, having stuffed my bag up on the luggage rack and pulled down the window to lean out and say goodbye to my friends, I was assailed by doubts. What was I doing, a girl of nineteen, from a small village in Lancashire, going on a tour of Europe with a Canadian rock band? I didn't know the answer and I was scared. I thought about getting off the train. I could have done.

I didn't have to go. But then what if I didn't? What would happen then? I didn't know the answer to that question either, and I was confident I didn't want to. What was there to be scared of? The unknown or not knowing the unknown? The latter, without a doubt, was the more frightening possibility. And so I waved goodbye as the train pulled out of the station, pushed up the window and took my seat.

I disembarked at Euston and took a cab to Blackheath where Lorraine lived. The next day we were to take a hire car and travel in convoy with the band. Merchandisers would travel separately to the band and load up their vehicles with stock. I would soon learn about the other items of luggage—huge amounts of cash stuffed into carrier bags—thousands of pounds in notes and coins of various currencies. During the one week touring with Elvis Costello, all I'd done apart from selling T-shirts was roll up posters. I realised that there was much more to merchandising than I had thought. I learnt about stock-taking, form-filling, budget-setting and forward-planning. My poster-rolling skills didn't go unexercised, however: as the youngest member of the merchandising team, I found myself sat on the floor tightly rolling hundreds of posters, securing them with elastic bands and sucking my paper-cuts.

I learnt about the dynamics of life on the road, how the camaraderie which prevailed at the beginning of a tour gave way after several weeks of close and constant proximity to bickering and bitchiness and outright belligerence. Relations could hardly have been helped by the wretchedness of our travelling conditions—the pervasive cigarette smoke which staled the interiors of the vehicles and everything in them, including the new merchandise; the wrappers, take-out trays, cups and cans strewn about, crammed in car doors and filling the footwells, the ashtrays overflowing with cigarette ends. After the shows we could escape to the cleanliness of our hotel rooms, only to return to the squalor in the morning as we got on the road to get to the next gig.

I was sharing a hotel room with Lorraine. She was in her thirties and I could tell she didn't like my youth, nor the attention I received because of it. From the outset she made it quite clear that she wasn't going to be my mother. (She was just about old enough to be so.) If she hadn't been so resentful of my presence, she might have thought to mention that I was eligible for a per diem to cover my living expenses. When she offered me the job, Eve must have presumed that I'd be aware of this. As it was, I wasn't. Nor did I know that I could eat the food provided for the band and crew. I lost a lot of weight. One night I stole a bottle of Coca-Cola from a hotel mini-bar for nourishment.

I had little time to worry about Lorraine or living expenses, however. Rush were, and are, a merchandising marvel, shifting more stock than any other band in history. The show would finish at eleven and we would still be selling merchandise at three in the morning. It didn't matter if we didn't have the right sizes—the fans just had to have the T-shirt to take away with them. If someone needed a size extra-large and all we had left was size small, they'd take the small. Meeting demand was a constant struggle. The manufacturers worked apace all day to produce the merchandise. For the second tour with Rush that I went on, Gerry Bron, of Bronze Records, used to loan us a plane so that each day the merchandise could be flown from the manufactory to the venue. The queues (I use the word loosely) were always enormous. If there was a group of friends wanting T-shirts, they'd usually designate one person to join the queue and buy them for everyone.

The worst queue I ever saw, also on my second tour with Rush, was at Deeside Leisure Centre, in Quensferry in Flintshire, North Wales. The ice rink had been covered over to make an auditorium. The main entrance had been closed off, the audience entering the building through the emergency exits along the side of the building opposite the front doors. This meant that the fans had to cross the auditorium to get to the foyer where we were selling the merchandise. The doors opened and the fans started to pour in, a queue quickly forming at the merchandise stalls. Before long the queue was so long that it had to wind through into the auditorium. We were selling quickly but not quickly enough. The queue now ran along the entire edge of the auditorium, blocking off the entrances through the emergency doors. The fans were asked to move out of the way of the doors, which they did, the queue growing as more fans streamed in, winding in on itself, maze-like, until it couldn't grow anymore: the auditorium had been completely taken over for the queue to buy merchandise. There were still fans outside, however, pushing their way in, the queue, with no possibility of extending, swelling instead. It got to the point where something had to give. And it did.

One moment, Lofty, one of the roadies was to my right, standing by a glass door connecting the foyer to the auditorium; the next he was under it, part of the back wall having collapsed against the force of the crowd on the other side. The fans, who till then had been getting increasingly impatient and noisy, only became more so as they pushed their way to the stall, stepping over the rubble. Things had got completely out of hand. Lurch, Rush's tour manager, squeezed through and told us that we would have to stop selling. We packed up the stall and the disappointed fans poured out of the foyer into the auditorium to watch the show. If we hadn't stopped selling they wouldn't have seen it; they'd have spent the entire night jostling to buy T-shirts.

Selling merchandise was exhausting work but a lot of fun. Though I couldn't call myself a fan, I loved being part of Rush's company. They weren't pompous or preening, though they had every right to be so given their extraordinary talents and such a dedicated following. With my tour pass, I was in the service of the priesthood. And once I discovered that I could partake of the breakfast, coffee and lunch provided by the caterers, I no longer had to worry about scrimping.

It was only later that I discovered the reason for Lorraine's resentment. A friend of hers had wanted the job I'd been given. So as not to be deprived of her company, she invited her friend to follow the tour across Europe. In Holland we had a couple of days off and Lorraine took off with her friend in the merchandising car, along with all my belongings, leaving me with no means of transport, no money and no change of clothes. Thankfully, there were others who looked out for me. I'd become friends with Geddy Lee's roadie, Skip, who was from the States and, at twenty-two, the youngest member of the road crew. Nothing happened between us, but because we were the youngest of our respective teams, we had something in common. I also got on well with one of the caterers and two guys from the lighting team. I think they accorded me a certain amount of respect because I was there to work, not to sleep with the band or crew. On the days off, when I had no money, others saw that I didn't go hungry. One night, when we arrived at a hotel, I found that a room hadn't been booked for me. I was going to sleep on the bus but someone booked me in. Life on the road certainly wasn't all tensions and tempers. Strong friendships are born of shared trials and, there being plenty of the latter, the former was a gratifying upshot.

By the time we reached Germany, halfway through the European leg of the tour, I was exhausted. I thought I must be ill. I was young and fit and up till then had been in good health, yet my stamina was dwindling while everyone else's seemed undiminished. How did Lorraine, in her thirties, manage to get up at the same time as me having gone to bed at four or five in the morning? I asked her how she did it and she took me to one side. Conjuring a small bag of white powder, she asked me if I'd ever tried coke. I said I hadn't. She cut me a line and I sniffed it up. All it did was block my nose and made me feel like I had a cold. She looked at me as if to say, did that answer my question? It didn't. How could this possibly be a substitute for sleep? I thought she must be mad. It was a disappointing initiation and it was a long time before I tried it again.

One of the things which makes festivals so much fun is that the various bands and their crews tend to stay in the same hotel, as was the case in Geleen. The night before the final show, we all went down to the bar. The Police were sat on a sofa off to one side. I went to order a drink and Sting joked to the barman that I was too young to be served. The barman looked at me. I could see he was in two minds about whether to serve me. He asked if I had any ID. I hadn't. Sting said he was only joking, he didn't know how old I was. 'How old are you?' he asked me. 'Twenty-one?' I said, rebuking myself for the upwards intonation. The barman said he was sorry but, without any ID, he couldn't serve me. Sting got up from the sofa, came to the bar and asked me what I'd like to drink. I said I'd have a rum and coke. Sting asked the barman for a rum and coke. The barman said he was sorry but he knew that that drink was intended for me and I hadn't presented any ID to show that I was of legal drinking age. 'Christ,' said Sting. 'Sorry about that, kid.'

A little pissed off that everyone else was getting pissed and I wouldn't be, I told Skip what had happened. Skip then told Geddy Lee, who went and hired a private room furnished with a bar and invited me to join the Rush crew to celebrate the end of the tour. In gratitude, I drank everything that came my way and was duly wrecked. Skip, Geddy and I left the party together. We went up in the lift and I stumbled out onto my floor, reaching the door and putting my key in the lock before crumpling to the carpet in a stupor. Geddy didn't reach his floor: he fell asleep in the lift. The next morning I woke in the hallway, my key still in the door to my room, the cleaner vacuuming around me. Geddy was still asleep in the lift, having spent the night travelling up and down, undisturbed by the considerate passengers.

Later in the day Geddy was revived and we made our way over to the venue. Usually with festivals, in order to reduce the amount of time spent setting the stage between the various acts, the stage is set in two halves—the band who is to play first at the front half of the stage, the band who is to go on after them at the back half, so the second band's equipment only has to be brought forward once the first's has been cleared away. The stage, as you'd expect for a festival, was very high, and, these being the days before health-and-safety, there was no back to it. One of the roadies, unmindful, took a step backwards and fell from the stage. There was a horrible thud and a cracking sound as he hit the floor. I ran over from where I had been at the side of the stage. Mick Jagger, who had been over on the other side, was there as soon as I was, asking the guy if he was okay, asking me if I knew who he was. I told him he was one of the roadies. Over Mick's shoulder, I saw Jerry Hall was there too. Mick asked her to get someone to call an ambulance. I couldn't believe it.

Mick Jagger. Right there. Kneeling with me beside the injured roadie, who was evidently in a lot of pain. This was no time for being starstruck. We stayed with him till the paramedics arrived and he was taken off on a stretcher. It turned out that he had broken his leg. Bad as this was, it could have been a lot worse.

*

The tour finished and I returned home. Alighting at Preston station in my Rush shirt, I took a cab straight to the high school where my mum worked and waited for her in the car park. I hadn't had any contact with her for the duration of the tour. Hugs over, she asked me how it had been. I told her. I also told her how much money I'd come back with: £1,300 in cash, in addition to the £15 per diems for six weeks that I hadn't received thanks to Lorraine—just a little short of £2,000 in all. My mum, having put up with I don't know what those weeks I'd been away ('Your daughter's doing *what*?' 'And you *let* her?'), marched back into school and told her cynical colleagues that her nineteen-year-old daughter had earned more money that month than the headmaster.

I was getting out.

2

Postcards from Europe

It was happening. My next tour. I was leaving village life behind for good. I knew this was what I wanted though I didn't know what to expect. I took an early train from Preston station, my destination the 'Holy T-shirts' offices at 15 Great Western Road. As I drew ever closer, it occurred to me that if I had any doubts about taking the job, now was the time to act on them. I didn't *have* to take it. I *could* go back. I could call the offices, tell them I'd changed my mind, I didn't want to tour anymore, apologise profusely and thank them kindly, then when I was back home I could begin to forget about it all, the embarrassment gradually fading while I...

While I what? What was there for me back in the village? What was there that I *wanted* back in the village? Scared as I was, I knew that I was much more scared of a life in slow-motion out in the provinces—a life of nine-to-five, cooking and cleaning, raising a family, waiting for the weekend... Yes: I was much more scared of that. These thoughts churning inside my head, the train pulled into

Euston station and I noticed a sign saying 'Take Courage' on the side of a pub. It might have been written just for me. If there was a trace of indecision left in me, it vanished then. Whenever I've been travelling on the line since, I've looked out for that sign.

When I got off the train, lugging my oversized suitcase, I realised I didn't know how to get to the offices. I called the telephone number I'd been given, explained who I was and asked for directions. Somehow I managed to find my way there, emerging from Westbourne Park tube station and, remembering to turn left, heading up Great Western Road. Passing over a canal bridge, looking at the pubs along the bank, I thought how this strange place would soon become familiar—provided I did a good job and I wasn't let go before it had chance. I carried on up the street, checking the house numbers as I went, and sure enough, there it was, number 15—a white stuccoed Georgian terrace, four floors including a basement. Apprehensive, I stepped up to the door, put down my suitcase and pressed the buzzer. A woman's voice came over the intercom and asked me who I was. I told her, there was a buzz and a click, and I entered the offices.

My very first impression was one of chaos. There were people bustling about with arms full of paperwork, running up and downstairs with parcels and boxes, popping up from the basement, questions and instructions shouted across the several floors. Lemmy and 'Fast' Eddie Clarke were there (though I had no idea who they were at the time), hanging around, looking a lot less flustered than everybody else. There were two reception desks, a sofa and a table. Behind one of the desks was a frightening-looking woman with long black hair, black eye make-up, a top that left but a very little to the imagination, the shortest miniskirt I had ever seen and a pair of thigh-length boots. It was later in the day that I learned the name she went by: Motorcycle Irene. Intimidated, I made myself go forward.

'So you're Kim?' she said as I stepped up to the desk.

Noticing with some puzzlement a strait jacket lying on top of it, I nodded. Following my gaze, she glinted amusement.

'Take a seat,' she said, indicating the sofa.

I sat down and watched the frenetics, my eyes constantly drawn to Motorcycle Irene as she talked with the guys from Motörhead. She caught my eye and I looked away. When I looked back, she was still watching me. I was feeling very uncomfortable.

Her eyes glinted again and she grabbed the strait jacket from the desk, flicking a look at the Motörhead guys.

'Come here,' she said, beckoning me with a finger.

Leaving my suitcase by the sofa, I went and stood before the desk.

'Try this on, would you?' she said. 'I'd like to see how it looks on you.'

I tried to work out whether she was joking. She didn't seem to be. I looked from her to the Motörhead guys. They nodded as if to say I should go ahead. I pulled the strait jacket on and Motorcycle Irene came round the side of the desk to tie it up at the back.

'Now try and get out of it.'

As I stood before her and the Motörhead guys, wriggling inside the jacket and realising immediately that there was no way I was getting out of it by myself, I felt like a rabbit caught in three sets of headlights. They were all very much amused, their faces creasing with laughter. I struggled vainly to release myself, my crimson face stark I'm sure against the white of the jacket. With only one chance when it comes to first impressions, I'd hoped to come across cool and cultivated and I was painfully aware I'd done anything but.

Mercifully, a buzzer sounded and a voice asked that I be sent up. Motorcycle Irene released me from the jacket and told me to go up to the top floor. She said I could leave my suitcase down there in reception. Though reluctant to leave it with them, there was no way I was going to lug it upstairs with me and make an even bigger fool of myself, so I left it and went to the stairs. Looking up the stairwell, I could see the top floor above. I reached the first floor and through an open door looked into an office containing a number of massive desks piled with paperwork, behind one of which was a guy poring over a mess of documents. Also in the room was a woman taking notes. A blonde, she was the opposite of Motorcycle Irene—just as striking, but much more glamorous. I carried on up to the top floor, where, through another open door, behind another overloaded desk, sat my new boss, Eve Carr.

I had been anxious about meeting her. Over the phone she had sounded brusque, aggressive even. I realised, however, that it was her Swedish accent that, sounding harsh to my ear, had led me to form this intimidating idea of her. Once we were introduced, she asked me to start sorting badges and patches into batches of a hundred and bag them up. The rooms were crammed with boxes of merchandise, so I found a piece of floor to sit on and set to work.

It soon got to lunchtime. It looked like everyone in the office was going to a pub on the canal, so I went along with them. (The other place to go for lunch was a tiny café across the road, where we went for coffee, breakfast and snacks during the day, as did many of our clients. There were only five or six seats and a bar running along one side. The walls were covered in signed photographs of its rock 'n' roll patrons.) Lunch lasted a good two hours, starting at 1 pm. Everyone was drinking—and drinking a lot. Double vodka-and-orange seemed to be the drink of choice. I don't know how many they must have got through between them. As far as I can recall, I wasn't drinking. I don't think I ate anything either, I was so nervous.

About 3 pm everyone started to wend their way back to the office. I'd thought with the amount everyone had taken on that the rest of the day would be written off—but no, there were barely any signs of boozy torpor; everybody carried on working with more or less the same energy as in the morning when the coffee maker had been constantly awhir. It was shortly after that I learnt that caffeine wasn't the only drug fuelling the office, its diuretic effects not sufficient to explain the frequency of the visits to the toilet between the ground floor and the first floor, where I noticed traces of white powder on various surfaces. I don't think it was ever actually used as a toilet.

As I became accustomed to the office, I realised that stimulants were essential to its functioning: the work simply couldn't have got done without them. There was no nine-to-five regularity. People would show up about 10 am and work until there was a moment not too inconvenient to leave. With bands touring all over the world, working in different time zones, crises would be flaring up twenty-four-hours. It was an unhealthy regime but the work had to be done and it was—not that you'd ever be able to tell from the mounds of paperwork which never seemed to get any smaller.

That's not to say, however, that everything always went smoothly. Eve Carr and Doug Smith—the man I had seen working on the first floor—used to bicker constantly. I know this, as did everyone else in the building, because I could hear them shouting at each other up and down the stairwell. Though all the offices on the different floors were connected by an intercom system, they always opted for this more strenuous means of communication. '*EVE...!*'

Doug would shout up. *'DOUGLAS...!'* Eve would shout down.

Accusations and lengthy tirades would follow, usually brought to an

end with an exasperated 'Oh fuck off!' I used to find this hilarious.

You would never have guessed that they were partners, Eve

and Doug. They had met in the States. Eve had been in the music

industry since she was very young. Doug had worked as a roadie for

various bands and climbed up through the ranks to own a number of

companies concerned with band-management, merchandising,

publishing, you name it. He owned a record company too. He was

well-known. So well-known, in fact, to have been an answer to a

Trivial Pursuit question ('Who was the original manager of the band

Motörhead?').

He had his own special methods of personnel organisation.

When it came to the female employees who dealt with clients and

customers—receptionists, merchandisers, etc.—he would always

make sure they worked in complementary pairs: a blonde and a

brunette—or at least a dark-haired girl (Motorcycle Irene, on

reception, definitely wasn't a brunette). Today employers would

probably be less blatant about employing such business stratagems,

but these were other days.

When it came to deciding who should work with which bands, he always put people with a band they didn't like. If you liked punk, you wouldn't work with The Damned. If you liked heavy metal, you wouldn't work with Motörhead. If you said you loved so-and-so, you were guaranteed that there was no chance of your ever working with them. I didn't like heavy metal. Motörhead did nothing for me. The leather, the facial hair—*eugh!* was my instinctive reaction. Hence, I ended up working with Motörhead. This was shrewd of Doug, as it meant you weren't distracted by adoration and got on with your job. It also discouraged groupieism: you were there to work, not to sleep with the band. I had no desire to sleep with any of the guys from Motörhead.

For all that I admired him, I was quite scared of Doug and did the best I could to stay out of his way lest I unleash his temper. When I was going out with my daughter Kennedy's father, who also worked for Doug, I was in London about to go off on a tour. Doug called me at my hotel and said that I was not to go in to the office that day and that he wanted to see me the next morning with my 'future husband' (this said in an ominous tone of voice) at 10 am sharp. It was all because he didn't agree with people going out with each other on tour and said he was put in an awful position as Motörhead wanted to keep my future husband as their lighting designer while Doug and Eve wanted to keep me because I made them more money. We were told to keep our distance while we were on tour. It was a real rap on the knuckles. I came to appreciate, however, that much of his severity with me was motivated by protectiveness. He became a sort of father-figure. Years later, when his son turned nineteen, he told me he couldn't believe that I'd been his son's age when I had come to work for him.

Working in the office, you never knew who might call or show up, usually to speak or meet with Doug, who looked after a number of bands. Business meetings would normally be held in his office but would fairly swiftly relocate to the pub. As with the Motörhead guys, you could generally tell by various cues—sartorial, attitudinal, auric—whether someone was a personality. The trouble I had was telling precisely *which* personality, which made for some awkward moments.

Everyone was always so busy, entirely absorbed in making arrangements and managing crises, never having time for a chat on the stairs or even to say hello. If there was a phone ringing, as there nearly always was, and there was no one else to answer it, I'd pick it up—usually after someone shouted at me to do so. I was always nervous doing this as it could be anyone at the other end, though that anyone would almost invariably be a someone. The caller would typically give only their first name, expecting whoever had picked up the phone to know just who it was that was calling. Sometimes they wouldn't even say their name, expecting their voice to establish their identity. Afraid of disappointing an ego, I didn't like to ask who it was, so I'd just put them through to Doug. When he asked me who it was, I'd tell him, sorry, I didn't catch the name, and he'd yell for the umpteenth time: 'Ask who it is *before* you put it through!'

One time in Los Angeles, I was staying at a guitar technician's house during a tour. It was quite common for members of the crew to stay at each other's houses as it meant a change to another pristine hotel room and restaurant dining—both things which I happened to love and couldn't imagine ever tiring of—and the host would be reimbursed by management. At this guitar tech's house, the phone rang. I picked it up and before I had chance to say hello, the caller asked to speak to the guitar tech. Wanting to sound professional and efficient, I said he wasn't available, could I take a message? 'Yeah, tell him Ritchie called.' 'Ritchie?' I said. 'Yeah, Ritchie, tell him Ritchie called.' It sounded like he knew the guitar tech but I didn't know whether the guitar tech would know who this Ritchie was. It was conceivable he might know other Ritchies. 'Ritchie who?' I fumbled. 'Ritchie Blackmore.' I'd never heard of him. Had the guitar tech? '*Did* you have a message, or should I ask him to call you back?' 'Just tell him Ritchie called.' The phone went dead. There were a lot of those sorts of conversations.

All day, every day, an endless barrage of problems would pour through the telephone receivers. 'So-and-so has gone missing.' 'Such-and-such has been arrested.' 'We've missed our flight.' 'We've run out of money.' So much of the time was taken up with crisis-management, and this was in addition to all the regular day-to-day work that had to be done.

There was one long stream of complaints from The Damned during a tour of Europe. A minivan had been hired as their transport and the band *hated* it. Apparently it was always breaking down. With their being the other side of Europe, this was a distant concern for those of us in the office. Until, that is, bits of the van started coming through the letterbox with the wodges of mail stuffed through each day. One day there would be a piece of metal, another day a visor, another a handle, each tagged with a note—something like: 'Having a lovely time. Wish you were here. The Damned.'

Another constant inconvenience for the company, though one which no one ever took any real notice of, was parking fines. It simply wasn't worth it to us. Each day on tour we would pay in the previous night's takings from the sale of merchandise, the amounts ranging from £2,000 to £20,000—in cash and stuffed into carrier bags. Usually two of us girls would go along to the bank. It was unlikely that anyone would suspect, dressed in jeans and trainers as we were, carrying a

couple of Sainsbury's bags, that we had such a lot of money on us. Each day we would eat breakfast, get ready, check out of the hotel and get to a bank to pay in the takings before closing time, allowing enough time to get to the next venue for between 3 and 4 pm. Because we didn't have much time and because we were responsible for such an obscene amount of money, we would park right outside the bank. Since we would be in there a while, we almost always ended up with a parking ticket. As merchandisers, a lot of the time we had to make our own way to the venues and usually there wouldn't be parking spaces for us. Often, we would just park up right outside the venue, allowing us to easily get back to the vehicles if we needed anything, incurring more parking tickets. On one tour we decorated the van with the parking tickets we were given, wallpapering the interior, the door panels, the ceiling all covered in the yellow slips.

One of the worst disasters, which thankfully I had nothing to do with, happened when I was on tour with Hawkwind. This was the time when programmes were becoming really expensive, more expensive than T-shirts. Fans could expect to pay £5 for one. Because of this, we'd barely sold any. Rather than lugging the boxes about for the remainder of the tour, it was decided to send them back to Great Western Road. One of the employees called Simon was deputed to collect them in the Ford Granada. He was my age, the two of us the youngest members of the office. We were always smiling, giggling, making mischief—partners in crime, but innocent ones. Simon drove out from London and met us somewhere in Europe. We loaded the boxes of programmes into the boot and he set off on his way back. Arriving in London in the early hours of the morning, he decided to take the Granada for a spin before returning to the office. He had a whale of a time, tearing round, imagining himself in *The Sweeney*. Unfortunately, however, he hadn't noticed that the boot hadn't shut properly. Someone phoned Doug Smith later that morning to tell him that there were

Hawkwind programmes strewn all down the Harrow Road. 'Can't you pick them up?' said Doug. 'No mate,' came the reply. 'There's like hundreds of them.' Simon being Simon, he was forgiven. It had been a costly mistake though. The next week, when Hawkwind were playing in London, the pirates were selling the official programmes outside the venues at half the price we were selling them inside. When the fans opened them up, however, they found that they were damaged, pages missing. The pirates were telling them to get them changed inside. So we had fans coming up to the stall, asking for us to change their mutilated programmes and complaining at our pricing. In the end we had to stop selling. Money-wise, it was a real blow.

*

Initially, when we were in London on tours, I would be put in rooms in cheap hotels. I used to hate this, living in these little rooms while everybody else was staying in swankier establishments or in their own digs in the city. I'd often spend the days-off alone in my room, no one to talk to or eat with, watching TV, eating Mars bars and drinking cans of Coke. And sleeping. We all accrued substantial sleep deficits. Sometimes I would make my way down to Hammersmith Odeon because there was bound to be someone there I knew working for whoever was playing that night. Doing that, I got to see people like Kate Bush and Peter Gabriel and many others, which made a fun way of passing the evening.

In Glasgow one time I was staying in a Holiday Inn with the rest of the band and crew. Rod Stewart happened to be staying on the same floor as me. He had members of his entourage who spent the entire day in each of the two lifts going up to that floor, making sure that the only people who got off on that floor were the guests who had rooms on it. I had a key slip to confirm that I was one such. It was 2 am and I got back to the hotel after the gig and went up in the lift. I stepped out into the corridor and found that it was blocked with flight cases, piled one on top of another. They had been left open. I could see they contained his and his wife's extensive wardrobes, the contents spilling out onto the floor. I had to climb over them to get to my room. The next day I happened to take the lift with him. To look at him, if I hadn't known he was staying there, I would have thought he was an American golfer—purple-and-yellow tartan trousers, a golfing sweater of the same colours and a flat cap. I said to him, 'With so much luggage I thought you'd be better dressed.' Cheeky, I know, but he laughed.

Later, I used to stay with another company employee called Jane. She had a flat in Westbourne Grove. If, say, there was a string of ten nights at the Hammersmith Odeon, I'd stay with Jane, along with some of the other merchandisers, and she would be paid by the company for sharing her flat with us. I felt a little intimidated and rather an imposition. Still, it was better than being alone in a poky hotel.

The most fun we had in the flat was with a green laser that had been left by a lighting technician. There was a pub at the end of the road and we used to mess with the drunks when they stumbled out, shining the laser at their feet and watching them stamp on it. We would point it into the flats on the other side of the road and watch the residents slapping their walls. That this was my fondest memory of those days gives you an idea how bored we used to get.

Another of the merchandisers with whom I got on well and often worked with on tours was called Janet. She was very well-spoken, cultured and elegant, and rather partial to a drink. One summer we went to Blackpool to sell merchandise for the Nolan Sisters, who were appearing at the Winter Gardens for six weeks. Three merchandising teams would work two-week stints. We had been allocated our own kiosk to sell from. The only trouble was, being some distance from the concert hall, no one knew that we were with the Nolan Sisters. Unsurprisingly, business was slow. Me, Janet and her boyfriend Mark were staying in a holiday apartment in St Annes. One evening, Janet and Mark had had a little too much to drink and an argument had flared up. Having gone over there for a holiday before my turn on the stall, knowing how their arguments tended to escalate, I thought I'd get out of the way. I could tell it wouldn't be long before they started throwing things. It was about midnight when I went down to the car park, got into my car, pulled out and reached the gate to find that the car park was closed for the night. I was stuck. I went back up to the apartment and found it trashed. Retiring to my bedroom, I tried to get some sleep and left the next morning. Business having been so bad, it was decided that there was no point us being there, so in the end my two weeks never came up.

One of my best friends was a girl my age called Kathleen who worked in the publishing department at 15 Great Western Road. It was one of those instant friendships and it made the time in the office much more fun. She didn't stay there as long as I did and went to New York to work for a publishing house. Some years later, I met up with her at her club when I was working on an American tour—one of those very exclusive institutions with lots of gleaming dark wood and plump leather upholstery—and we drank whisky as we used to do when we were working together in London, though the whisky we were drinking this time was rather a lot better than the last. The way the room started rolling when I stood up to go to the ladies confirmed the time that had passed since we last had a drink together. Balancing with my arms, I navigated the room and tried to ignore the pairs of eyes lifted out of brandy balloons and martini glasses as I walked past, their owners apparently well aware that I wasn't a member. I was perhaps dressed a little out of the club's ordinary—an all-in-one jumpsuit and waistcoat jacket. I returned a few minutes later minus the jacket which I had somehow managed to drop into the toilet basin. I had considered my options—lift it out or leave it—and decided on the latter. After a few frantic attempts to flush it down, I gave up and made a swift exit before anyone else came in.

By this time, I was enjoying my work a lot more. Having moved up the ladder, I was given rooms in better hotels. One of these was the Columbia in Lancaster Gate, on the northern edge of Hyde Park. A Red Cross hospital during World War I and the London Officers' Club of the United States Air Force from the mid-50s, when it was known as the Columbia Club, the building became a hotel in 1975. Everyone in rock 'n' roll stayed there. Another rock 'n' roll hotel was the K West. The main reason bands ended up staying in the same places was that they all used the same travel agents. At the Columbia you could spend all night drinking in the bar and you could guarantee there would be someone you knew staying there. Tour crews made a small family, personnel going on tour with one band then on tour with another, so the same people would always show up. Another favourite hotel was the

Southampton Park Hotel (now closed)—not very big, nice rooms, quite old-fashioned—much better than the characterless corporate hotels which were always a nightmare to check out of. Even going to see the manager would take an hour. In the swankier places, we'd sometimes receive invitations to breakfast from the management. A pleasant gesture, except not that appealing when breakfast was served pretty much when you were going to bed.

*

Working under Eve and Doug at Great Western Road was the best preparation I could have had for my later career. Some years later, after my daughter was born, Chumbawamba were appearing for a Gay Pride parade in America. I needed to speak to the organisers and they said they would only talk after 4 am (my time). I'd had enough and was wanting some downtime. This was the final straw and I told Doug I was quitting. 'No you're not,' he told me. I waited for him to tell me why. He asked me where was I going to get a job which would pay me so well, afford me such a lifestyle and deliver as much excitement. I saw he had a point, and I stayed. I'll always be grateful to him. We're still in touch, both having left the music industry.

Though it was a bloody nightmare at times, I can look back at those early days working for Eve and Doug as some of the very best. I had known madness and kept my head, all that I'd learnt tucked away for when I walked into other offices—those of Capital Records, Variety, EMI, the William Morris Agency—working with the A&R people there. I'd know a lot more madness in the years to come. That, by and large, I managed to keep it together had a lot to do with Eve and Doug and the other members of their eccentric company.

*

Some years later, I was at a Rolling Stones concert in Copenhagen. My second husband was working as part of the crew, while I'd just gone along to see the show. Backstage was thick with personnel—talking, animated, bustling about. I felt completely out of it all. One of those times when you feel like you're running on a different set of tracks to everybody else.

'Hello, Kim.'

'Neil! Hi!'

It was Neil Warnock, the music agent. I'd had no idea he would be there. He had recognised me from the office at Great Western Road. Immediately I felt like I was back on a common plane. We started talking. It was a pleasure to see him again. It had been the sort of situation in which you'd give anything to glimpse a familiar face, and there Neil's had been—another little reason I had to be grateful for my time at Great Western Road.

3

Driven to Distraction

Life on the road isn't as fun as it sounds—just because so much of the time *is* spent on the road. Mostly it's tedious, often it's irksome and sometimes it's plain scary. It's one thing to get a show on the road, quite another to keep it there. Yet whatever the obstacle, however insuperable it might seem, you have to get to the next venue. Not arriving simply isn't an option.

*

Although when I started touring, road safety laws were more relaxed than they are now, they weren't so relaxed as to permit some of the ways we found to while away our journeys. I remember one time soon after I started out, driving to a gig with Janet in a minivan when we were touring with Gamma. Janet reached down into a carrier bag stowed in the footwell and pulled out a bottle of brandy.

'Drinkypoos?'

Because we earned good wages and received generous per diems, this wasn't Three Barrels she was offering; it was Rémy Martin XO.

'Not just now, thanks,' I said. I looked at the clock on the dashboard. It was barely ten o'clock in the morning.

'Just a little snifter?'

'Maybe later,' I said.

She dipped into the bag again and brought out a pair of balloon glasses.

'Pull alongside the other van, would you.'

This was the crew van carrying the band's equipment, just ahead of us. I pulled across into the outer lane and edged up alongside. Janet wound down the window, gesturing for the van driver to do the same. One hand keeping her wind-whipped hair out of her face, she held up the bottle and called across, 'Drinks, darling?' I was watching the road and the other van, careful to keep alongside. 'Get a bit closer, would you?' she said to me, pouring two generous measures without spilling a drop. I moved closer, only a yard or so between the two vans. Janet thrust a glass out of the window. 'Here, darling!' she sang. The driver reached down with his right hand, his left on the wheel and took the glass. 'Cheers!' They clinked glasses and took a swig. I restored the distance between the two vehicles.

'Sure you won't join us?'

I said I was sure.

Brandy wasn't the only thing that was passed between vehicles. I remember once with a friend called Jane, another of the merchandisers at Great Western Road, sharing lines of coke while we were driving through Jedburgh along the A68 on the way to Edinburgh. This was on a tour with Sammy Hagar. In the merchandise minivan, we pulled alongside the band minibus, windows were wound down and lines of coke were cut on a compact mirror and passed across from one vehicle to the other. The only trouble was, hurtling along at the speed we were, the coke was whisked away by the wind before it got anywhere near our noses. If we'd been thinking straight, we would have realised it was a physical impossibility to transfer lines of coke intact across vehicles while travelling at fifty miles-an-hour. Only we weren't thinking straight; we were completely out of it.

Whilst this was all of course in contravention of road safety laws, we had a sense that the rules just didn't apply to us. Firstly, this had to do with the money we had behind us: if we did get into any trouble, it was likely we'd be able to pay our way out of it. Secondly, it had to do with the fact that in those days you were unlikely to be noticed. There were no cameras, patrolling was lighter. If you were ever spotted doing something you shouldn't be, chances were that you'd be able to outspeed the police. If we didn't need the van, we'd travel in a Ford Granada. Bands would often go and buy themselves some very hot wheels. Geezer Butler of Black Sabbath, who had made a packet with their album *Paranoid*, had a Rolls Royce at eighteen. Whatever you found yourself caught up in, the show had to go on, and it did.

On one occasion we were stopped, however. We were driving down the M4, over the toll bridge. It was pouring with rain. We were travelling in a Transit van and Jane was driving, driving fast. She was smoking a joint too. The merchandise was piled high in the back of the van, blocking the rear windows. We therefore heard the police car before we saw it.

'Shit,' said Jane, snatching the joint from her mouth. 'Here, get rid of it.'

'How?' I said, panicking.

'Throw it out the window.'

The police car pulled alongside, the officer looking across and indicating that we should pull over. Jane nodded vigorously, leaning forward in her seat while I wound down the window and chucked the joint out of it.

'It blew back in!' said Jane.

'What?'

'The joint, the joint—it blew back in!'

I twisted round in my seat, looking for it.

'Oh Jesus,' said Jane, pulling in to the side of the road. She cut the engine. 'Have you found it?'

'No,' I said. I couldn't see it anywhere.

'Leave it,' said Jane. 'He's coming over.'

The policeman was out of his car, shrugging on his coat and hunching his shoulders against the lashing rain. Jane wound down her window and the policeman thrust his head through to shelter it.

'Hey,' said Jane, 'you're getting me all wet.'

'Oh, beg your pardon,' he said, dipping his head and tipping water from the top of his cap. Jane shifted over in her seat. The officer retreated into the rain, water pouring from the brim of his cap like a waterfall.

'What have I done, officer?' said Jane, batting her long blonde eyelashes.

'You were driving in excess of the speed limit and in a dangerous fashion.'

'Was I? Did you think so, Kim?'

'Hm?' I had found the joint, a little tape of smoke disclosing its location somewhere amidst the bags of T-shirts. 'No,' I said. 'No, I didn't think so.'

The officer demurred and Jane flirted placatingly, meanwhile I kept looking to the back of the van. The joint was no longer the only thing that was burning back there. Soon the smell of melting plastic drifted through to the cab.

'What's that smell?' said the officer.

'What smell?' said Jane, wrinkling her nose at the poisonous fumes.

'There's something burning in your van.'

'There is? Kim, can you see what it is?'

'I think it's a cigarette,' I said.

'Well put it out!' said the officer.

I clambered through to the back of the van. There were bags burning, T-shirts blackening within. After a lot of stamping around, the fire was extinguished. I clambered back through to the cab. The officer, sopping wet, didn't look pleased. He opened his mouth but Jane preempted him with an explanation of her erratic driving: I had been smoking a cigarette, had chucked it out of the window and it must have blown back inside the van. She added that, if she had been driving in excess of the speed limit, she was truly most terribly sorry and wouldn't let it happen again. Jane's flirtations, in combination with the deluge, proved effective: the officer allowed us to be on our way and hurried back to his car.

*

Having been driven through a great many countries, I can say without doubt that the best drivers are German. Some years later, I was working as a troubleshooter for the Elvis Presley impersonator

James Brown (aka 'the King'). He had won an award and his management at EMI thought he should go and collect it. The event would be broadcast on television and he would sing a number too. His management knew how difficult Jim could be, the reason being that he simply didn't like making appearances. On this occasion, however, there had been no asking Jim if he'd be willing. Management had decided: he was doing it. I thought this was absolutely the right thing to do.

I didn't think the same, however, about the treatment of Jim's band, who wouldn't be

appearing with him. Another band would be brought in. I decided that this wasn't on and said that the whole band needed to appear with Jim—if only to keep them together as resentment was starting to build between them. It was a last-minute decision and transport had to be rearranged. It was already a super-tight schedule: we had to get to the studios, Jim and the band would do their thing and then we would have to get to the venue for that evening's show. We hired a Lear jet to get us to the television studios. We arrived in time, Jim accepted his award, performed with the band and we hurried off.

Back in the air, time pressing, it started snowing—lightly at first, then in great fat flakes. I was beginning to think we wouldn't make the gig. We touched down at the airport, the last plane to land that evening, and stepped down into a foot-thick carpet of snow. I was almost certain we wouldn't make the gig. Until, that is, we were directed to a set of sleek saloon cars, a German driver behind each wheel, the fleet organised by the people at EMI. We bundled into the cars. I was in one with Jim. The driver told us to fasten our seatbelts. Jim said he didn't like to wear his seatbelt. 'I am not going to drive until you have put on your seatbelt,' said the driver politely but firmly. Jim acquiesced, and with a spin of wheels the driver lurched out of the airport, the other two cars behind, police escorts at the front and at the rear.

Talk about putting the pedal to the metal.

With our heads pressed back against the headrests, the driver doing handbrake turns round corners, I thought we were surely going to die. I soon relaxed, however, once I realised we were in the hands of an expert. We got a call from the police car in front telling us we should go on without them as they were slowing us down. We arrived at the venue forty-five minutes late. Jim and the band had to go onstage straightaway. The crowd were restless and a riot would likely have started if the show hadn't begun immediately.

These German racers were exceptional. Then again, that's what the circumstances had called for. Much of the driving on tours is done at ordinary speeds for extraordinarily long slogs. When I was working as a merchandiser and later as a tour manager, tachographs had been introduced to monitor the length of time a driver spent at the wheel, only they weren't very reliable. There was a drink that was popular with the drivers called Rocket Fuel. I'm not sure what was in it but the drivers used to swear by it. One guy drove for two-and-a-half days, stopping only to eat.

The journeys being so long, we were constantly seeking ways to alleviate the inevitable boredom. There were lots of drinking games—and when we'd had enough of those, just drinking. We'd buy bottles of whatever we liked at duty-free, get on the bus and stick in a straw. As a precaution against overindulgence you'd have a carrier bag in your bunk with you. This wasn't only for expediency: the bus's chemical toilet couldn't handle solids. One of the (really quite unpleasant) ways drivers had of retaliating against reckless motorists was by pulling in front of them and unloading the contents of the septic tank onto the road. Funnier for us, I'm sure.

Some of our diversions were more sporting. Bus surfing, for instance. This involved taking a metal briefcase (a Halliburton—the 'in' thing which you would invariably see handcuffed to the wrists of tour managers—a neat little advertisement to anyone who might be interested that that was where all the money was), placing it in the aisle near the front of the bus and then, with the help of the headrests either side, climbing on top, and, letting go of all supports, staying as long as you could on top of the briefcase. On the long straight motorways of Europe, where there were no speed-limits, the sensation was very like surfing a wave. (On British motorways—not so long or straight, with speed-limits and cameras—it wasn't the same.) There was an element of danger too: if you fell forward, which was quite likely if the driver braked, you'd fall straight into the windscreen.

Other pastimes were more staid. One of these was 'Tom Jones Bingo'. This game was invented by Johnette Napolitano, lead singer of Concrete Blonde. It was regular bingo with Tom Jones playing through the stereo. I can't quite remember how Johnette thought it up but before very long it was a thing. 'Let's play Tom Jones Bingo,' someone would say. 'Tom Jones Bingo, anyone?' We'd gather round with our cards and pencils and the Tom Jones compilation would be stuck in the player. Johnette insisted on everybody playing and, bad as it sounds, it was actually a lot of fun. Johnette probably enjoyed it the most of anyone: she nearly always won. Why, I don't know. She said she was lucky.

It was perhaps for this reason that she always wanted to stop at the Primm Valley Resort & Casino just before the Nevada state line when on our way back to LA along the I-15. Nobody else wanted to stop there as they were eager to get home after the tour. The bus would be making enough stops anyway, dropping off equipment in storage and members of the band and crew at their homes along the way. Johnette therefore asked me to hire a car for her so that she could stop at Primm and get home afterwards. She wanted to pay in cash, this being a personal expenditure. The only problem was I didn't have my driving license on me. I had only my passport and the band's credit card (not under my name). I explained this to the man behind the desk at the car hire centre having told him that I wanted to hire a car. 'You're English?' he said. 'Yes,' I replied. 'Can I see your passport?' I handed it over. 'That's fine,' he said, and gave me some papers to sign. It turned out that an English passport was as good as a driving license, regulations being much tougher in England than in the States. This wasn't some rinky-dink establishment either. I can't remember which, but it was the branch of a major car-hire company. Only in America, I thought, as I drove out.

Some of our bus drivers liked to pimp out their vehicles. In the case of one driver, it looked like her vehicle wasn't the only thing she was pimping. Her bus was all white inside, the seats white leather, the whiteness reflected in the mirrored ceiling. The aesthetic was unmistakably 70s porno. She wore jeans and a leather waistcoat and her grey hair in a ponytail. She must have been somebody's grandma. Her name was Missy J.

Most disturbing was the time I was woken by a member of the crew on an overnight drive and told that the driver was doing something at the wheel that he really shouldn't be. 'What?' I asked. The crew member shook a pale head and insisted with their eyes that I go and do something. I got out of bed and made my way to the front of the bus. I took a deep breath, preparing myself for whatever it was that I was about to find behind the curtain and pulled it aside. On a portable television he'd stuck up on his dashboard, the volume turned down low, the driver was watching I didn't know just what, though it was obviously something carnal, one hand holding the steering wheel, the other holding something else. I yanked the curtain back across and told him in no uncertain terms that he must stop doing at least one of the things he was doing *immediately*. He carried on driving. I trusted he'd stopped doing the other thing; I wasn't going to risk checking. Shuddering, I tried to expunge the image from my mind and went back to my bunk. He never drove for us again.

*

I was in Los Angeles where Concrete Blonde were on a short warm-up tour. They were appearing as Dream 6, this being the original name of the band formed by Johnette Napolitano and guitarist James Mankey in the early 80s (the change of name was suggested by R.E.M.'s Michael Stipe). Jim had played guitar for Sparks on their first two albums, as had his brother, Earle Mankey.

Sparks was another of the bands I'd watched as a teenager on Top of the Pops, as was Roxy Music, for whom Concrete Blonde's drummer Paul Thompson had played. Despite the years I'd spent in the industry, coming into contact with a host of artists, I still got a thrill from starry connections. Because fans generally don't want to hear new material but the hits—something bands hate ('We have to play this song *again*?')—reverting to the old name of Dream 6 meant that these would be lower-key gigs to which only the hardcore fans, who would be more receptive to new material, would turn up.

After the final show, to which the band's manager Frank Volpe had come along, Johnette said she wanted to go back in his car rather than the minibus we had been using. The other two band members said they would rather go back with Frank too. Frank said this was ridiculous, everyone going in his car but for me in the minibus, and offered to drive the minibus instead. I could drive his car. Johnette said no, she would rather go in the car. Frank was resolute, however, and they all got on board the minibus and I took his car. 'Just don't hit anything,' Frank told me as he dropped the keys into my palm. It turned out that the reason Johnette was so keen to go in the car was that she had left her dog in the minibus and it had shit *everywhere*. Apparently the smell was appalling. In an effort to combat it, Johnette had the idea of throwing coffee all over the faeces in order to cover the smell. I heard this made little improvement.

Meanwhile, I was enjoying driving Frank's car. Heading down Hollywood Boulevard, I took in the buildings with their flashing neon signs and the nightlife passing along the palm-lined star-set streets, my distraction so complete that I did the one thing Frank had told me not to do: I hit something. I couldn't believe it. I sat staring at the car in front of me and looked along the bonnet to try and see how much damage I'd done. I waited for the driver to get out, praying it wouldn't be Johnnie Crazy. No one got out. The car carried on driving and as it pulled away I saw I'd made a noticeable dent in the car's rear. I sat there a moment longer, staring, my heart still going, and then became aware of the cars behind me. I started the engine and drove on. I couldn't understand why the driver hadn't stopped. It had been quite a bump and they would most definitely have noticed. It was some time after that I heard there'd been a spate of thefts around the city involving cars being rear-ended and their drivers robbed when they got out. This is the only reason I could think of why I had been spared a confrontation. I wasn't complaining.

Speaking of bumps, when I was starting out as a merchandiser, I had to catch a plane from Heathrow. Not knowing how to get there, Mike Stuart (the promoter's agent who took me backstage to meet Elvis Costello) said he was driving past on his way to a gig and I could follow him. He was driving his boss John Curd's car—an orange and black Ford Escort 2000. John had a number of cars which he owned or rented and used to travel to various gigs, and this was his favourite.

Mike pulled up in the car park, an empty space adjacent. I nosed in, misjudged the angle and went into John's car. I jumped out and ran round to see what damage I'd done. My car was unscathed but there was a severe dent in the Escort which John would definitely notice. Mike told me not to worry about it, he'd explain to John, I should get checked in else I would miss my flight. Thanking him, I reversed and made a second attempt at parking, my forehead almost pressed against the windscreen, desperate not to hit the car again. I didn't, got out, got my bags and made my way to the terminal, apologising again and asking him to convey my sincerest apologies to John. Apparently (so I learnt when I got back), Mike had told John that someone had gone into the car at the gig that night. Uneasy as my conscience was, I never owned up.

It was surprising that more, and worse, such things, didn't happen to John. He did a lot of driving, and was always on the road with his work. He never kept to the speed limit and had an acute aversion to roadworks, which he ignored completely: he'd simply drive straight through them or use the hard shoulder to get round them.

If the police did catch you out, chances were, if you were driving a fast car (as people in rock 'n' roll almost invariably were), you could evade them. I remember hearing that Tony Iommi from Black Sabbath had been caught speeding in a sports car he'd just bought. The police chased him all the way from the London showroom to his Birmingham home. Not quite all the way home, though—he managed to lose them on the way. By the time the neighbourhood was roused by the flashing lights and sirens, he was tucked up in bed fast asleep. This wouldn't ever happen now, police vehicles not having such horsepower handicaps.

*

One time I was in Berlin for a one-off gig. We had a few days off and so me and my friend Jan decided to explore the city. Since we wouldn't be making much money with the gig, we didn't want to spend a lot, so we decided to see the city on roller skates, which was tremendous fun. One night we decided to go into East Berlin, which meant going through Checkpoint Charlie. There were two ways through the checkpoint, one for vehicles, the other for pedestrians. Since using the latter would mean having to go upstairs and across the footbridge to the other side, Jan and I decided that we would go the other way.

We were rolling through the checkpoint behind a car when we heard the American guards behind us shouting for us to come back. Ahead of us, the German guards raised their machine guns and pointed them straight at us. A shouted exchange followed between the Americans and Germans. Eventually agreement was reached: Jan and I would remove our roller skates and walk (in our socks) over into East Berlin via the footbridge. Later that night, on the way back, the American guards let us roll through with the cars. We had our picture taken and stuck up in the office.

I was in Berlin again, with Hawkwind, when the Berlin Wall came down. We'd been sent the address for the venue by the promoter. The journey had gone smoothly and we were approaching the venue when we found that we were quite suddenly and inexplicably lost. We drove around looking for the venue, checking the street signs and those of the establishments we passed. Running out of time and having seen no sight of it, we pulled over and someone jumped down to ask a waiting taxi driver if he could direct us. The driver had no idea where the venue was. We went on, asking taxi drivers, pedestrians, barmen. Eventually we had luck. It turned out that one of the first things that had been done after the collapse of the Wall was a jubilant rechristening of the streets in what had been East Berlin. We had been given the new address for the venue. The trouble was that the street signs hadn't been changed.

Later in the tour we were driving through Vienna, heading out of the city. It was early in the morning, about 2 am. All the band were in bed and I was sat at a table at the front of the bus, a few members of the crew still up too. We had stopped at a set of traffic lights. One moment I was in my seat at the table. The next I was across the table having slammed into the seat in front. It was several bewildered moments before I realised what had happened, and several more before I gathered myself up. Being responsible for the safety of the band and crew, I hauled myself along the bus and made sure that everyone was alright. Everybody wasn't alright but no one was dead or severely injured, though the driver looked like he needed medical attention. I told everyone to get off the bus and we spilled out on to the street. I saw then that the front of the bus had been shifted by about a foot, a silver Mercedes having gone through a red light and smashed into it.

A couple of guys walking down the street made their way over. They looked to be in their fifties with greyish-whiteish hair. I'm not sure where they were from but I presumed they were Austrian, since they spoke it. The spoke English too, with an American accent. I was so relieved, having wondered just what we were going to do at that time in the morning with only a few Austrian words between the lot of us. They offered to call the emergency services on our behalf, one of them going off to do so. He came back a few minutes later to tell us that ambulances were on the way. They arrived promptly and while the bus driver and the driver of the Mercedes were lifted onto stretchers I asked myself what the rest of us, for the most part unscathed, only shaken up, were going to do. The bus was at a busy junction, completely undriveable, its front bashed in. I suggested that everyone get back on it. Though the equipment wasn't stowed on board, all our personal belongings were. The Austrians were looking over the bus and even stepped up to poke their heads inside. I asked if they could take me to the phone they had used to call the ambulance so I could call management to see what we should do. They said sure, it wasn't far, they would take me there. I asked one of the crew to come with me.

We walked a short way to a bar. It was a seedy joint, in keeping with that part of Vienna. I was shown where the phone was, thanked the Austrian guys, and called the office, lightly holding the receiver with as few fingers as possible and careful not to let it touch my hair. It was decided that the band should check into a hotel while the crew would be asked to sleep on the bus to make sure that nothing was stolen, for which they would be paid extra. The gig for the following night would be cancelled and the band would be flown to the next town the following day. I and the crew would follow by sleeper train.

I replaced the phone and brushed my hands and went back through to the bar area where the other crew member was waiting. The Austrians asked what we intended to do. I told them. They said they knew the hotel we were to stay at, it was a good one. We were about to leave the bar when they said they had something to show us. I asked them what. Just come this way, they said, beckoning. I hesitated, wary. I glanced at the man behind the bar smoking a cigarette, drooped over a newspaper, offering no indication whether I was right to feel apprehensive. I looked to the crew member and he shrugged his shoulders. I said we'd better be getting back to the bus soon. They said that was alright, it would only take a moment.

We followed them to the rear of the bar. A curtain was pulled aside to reveal an ill-lit room, fusty and smelling of cigarette smoke, marijuana, high-proof spirits and unwashed bodies. People were lolling and lying on the floor, on chairs, on tables, many of them asleep. It was disgusting. Who were they all? I thought. And why did these Austrians want to show us them? I don't remember just what was said or how it was that I came to realise why the guys had been so interested in the bus: we were being introduced to a people-smuggling operation. I took a last unlingering look around and said that we had better be getting back to the bus. Come back later, one of the guys said. I said we would, knowing we wouldn't, thanked them for showing us the phone and made a vague signal of appreciative interest in their merchandise. We went back through the bar and out onto the street, not looking back.

We took taxis to the hotel, the crew having agreed to stay with the bus. Exhausted, we all went to bed. I woke early the next morning and went downstairs to see if I had any messages. I was told by the desk clerk that an Austrian gentleman had called and left a message for me, two messages in fact. He wanted me to call him back. Needless to say, I didn't, having no interest in helping him extend his operations by using the tour bus for people-trafficking. Of course you know such things go on but it's something else to be directly confronted with a proposition like that. I was glad to leave the city, though I felt guilty I hadn't done something, or even tried to do something, that I'd left those guys to find another conveyance for their human goods. But then, what was I to do? We made it to the next gig, the sleeper a nice change and thankfully both drivers recovered fully from their injuries.

*

For all the frustrations, tedium and sheer unpredictability, life on the road was out of the ordinary and this suited me just fine. Touring with Motörhead, however, was something else. I'll be saying more about my time with the band in the next chapter. Before coming to that though, I thought to finish this chapter by recounting some of the wilder journeys I made with them.

I was making my own way to one of their gigs in Rio de Janeiro, flying from Manchester to Paris, then from Paris to Rio. I got on the plane at Manchester and as we were approaching Charles de Gaulle airport one of the Air France flight attendants asked over the tannoy who was flying to Rio. I raised my hand with about a dozen other passengers. The attendant asked would we please collect our bags and go to the back of the plane. Picking up our bags, we did as we were asked. The attendant drew the curtains, screening us off from the cabin, and asked us to put down our bags, bend our knees and place our hands above our heads, we were coming in to land. Nervous glances were exchanged and we did as we were told. The attendant explained that there were significant delays at Charles de Gaulle due to Paris Fashion Week and that if we were to catch our flight to Rio we would need to be the first off the plane. (I need hardly say, health and safety regulations being as they are, there's no chance we would have been extended this courtesy today.)

The plane touched down, we rocked and swayed, one mohair-suited businessman rolling over and gathering himself up, and unbent our knees as the plane taxied down the runway. The attendant, not a hair out of place, apologised for the inconvenience and checked that we had our bags. 'Oh hell, my bag!' said a woman. 'You do not have your bag?' said the attendant. 'No, it's still in the overhead compartment,' the woman replied. The attendant nodded deprecatingly and said, 'This way, please,' then to the rest of us: 'Please wait here.' The plane had reached the gate by this point and the other passengers were getting their luggage down and making their way to the exit. 'Excuse me, please!' the attendant called ahead of her, squeezing her way down the aisle, the witless woman following behind. *'Excusez moi, s'il vous plaît!'* We ended up being the last off the plane.

Mercifully, we caught the plane to Rio, the captain having waited for us. What we didn't know was that an unscheduled stop had been announced shortly before we embarked. It was a night flight and, exhausted after all the bustling through the heaving terminal at Charles de Gaulle, I intended to get a good sleep. I nestled into my chair, wrapped myself in a blanket, wrote 'Please do not disturb' on a piece of paper and drifted off.

When I awoke, I looked out of the window and saw Christ the Redeemer illuminated on its dark hillside. Congratulating myself on my impeccable timing, I unwrapped myself and got my belongings together, preparing to land. The plane touched down, taxied to the gate and I got off with the other passengers who had assembled by the rear door to make a swift disembarkation—all sharply-dressed businessmen with briefcases.

I went to the baggage carousel and waited for my suitcase. The businessmen collected their bags and the attendant switched off the conveyor belt. I hadn't got my bag, nor had the other non-businessmen waiting with me. The attendant looked at us all, bagless. 'Our luggage?' someone said. His eyes widening, the attendant's jaw tightened, he bared his lower teeth and opened fire on us in Portuguese. Obviously we'd done something to upset him, but not speaking a word of Portuguese, I had no idea know what. Eventually we were told this wasn't Rio de Janeiro. An unscheduled stop had been made to drop off twelve oil men. I realised then that what I had thought was Christ the Redeemer spot-lit must have been the aeroplane wing light.

'Can we get another flight?' someone asked. We were told that we would have to wait two weeks for the next flight to Rio. That would be much too late. I asked an attendant if I could hire a car. 'A car?' they queried. 'To drive to Rio,' I said. 'You cannot drive to Rio from here.' 'Can't?' I said. I'd forgotten that the Amazon jungle was in the way. I was about to ask about hiring a plane when we were told that the plane had turned around and was on its way back to collect us. It was very embarrassing. I laughed with the attendant I'd asked about hiring a car as he explained that you would need boots and a machete to hack your way through swathes of unmarked territory to get to Rio from where we were and that you would probably need a more muscular vehicle than the standard hire Fiat

Uno. The flight crew, when they arrived, weren't nearly so jovial. The stewardesses gave us dirty looks and didn't give us another drink. Unpleasant as it was, it was much better than trying to penetrate the Amazon jungle in a Fiat Uno.

We arrived safely, if a little late, at Rio airport. I'd arranged to stay with a friend who lived in the city. On our day off she suggested we go and see the sights. Having decided to go by bus, we were waiting at a bus stop opposite a cornfield. As I was looking down the road, heat shimmering off the tarmac, out of the corner of my eye I saw the stalks part as a tall dark man emerged from them and walked up onto the road. It was immediately obvious that something wasn't quite right with him. He was moving slowly, his eyes rolled back in his head. He looked like a zombie and he was walking towards us. Had he seen us? Was he dangerous? Might he be undead? There didn't seem to be much going on inside his head and what there was I didn't want to know. We stepped aside. He walked straight past us, off the road and into the field opposite. As he disappeared into the distance and the bus pulled up, I looked at the driver smiling behind the wheel and his loud-chattering passengers and felt reassured by these bright signs of life.

On the flight back from Rio I sat next to the most remarkable woman. We got talking and she told me how, at the age of twelve, she had started working as a prostitute in order to survive on the streets of Rio. Early on, she said, when she was selling herself, she knew she had to turn things around. With high-powered businessman as clients, she had set about learning other languages—seven, in fact. She was fluent in all of them and had made a lot of money. Now she was bound for Germany where she had got a job as a translator. She was only nineteen.

The plane touched down and we said goodbye. Normally I would have changed on the plane. Snow was falling in Paris. As it was, my winter clothes were still in my hold-all, so I got off the plane in my shorts and T-shirt, looking every bit the dim tourist. Also in my hold-all was a bottle of a Brazilian sugar-cane liqueur which I'd brought back for some friends who had a taste for such dangerously high-proof tipples. When I went to get changed in the airport toilets I found that the bottle's seal had broken. My clothes reeked of alcohol. Rather than risk perishing of cold, however, I decided to put them on anyway.

It was while I was getting my clothes out that I noticed my backstage pass. This was very bad. Customs officials knew that backstage passes were often used by band members and crew for cutting lines and therefore scrutinised them for powder traces. If customs found the pass, it was a dead cert I'd be detained. Looking back on it, I should perhaps have dropped it in a bin. As it was, I took a more cunning precaution by making a list of all the things I'd brought back with me from Brazil, adding up the cost of the duty and walking through 'Something to declare'. I gave the list to the customs officer, who after a quick perusal told me I owed £5.50. As I'd hoped, he didn't look through my bag, I paid the sum and walked straight through.

*

It was worryingly easy to lose people on tour. With Motörhead, more so. We were travelling to Europe and, having taken the ferry to Calais, regrouped once we had disembarked— nearly all of us, that is. 'There's Würzel!' someone pointed. There he was, waving his arms at us from the top deck as the ferry began its return to England. We waited the several hours it took for the ferry to get to Dover and back to Calais, the next leg of the journey considerably less leisurely than it should have been.

Another night we left a roadie at a service station. The tour manager said he would have to find his own way, which was easier said than done when he had no money with him, just the clothes he was wearing. I thought this was awful. Later, when I was tour-managing myself, I always made sure I knew just who was and wasn't on the bus, getting up whenever we made a stop and checking that they were back on board before we set off. Inconvenient as this was, it was much more so than leaving someone behind, especially when we were travelling in America over such long distances when journeys might take several days.

*

Amongst other extravagances, Motörhead were well-known for their incredible stage sets, which really were incredible. A lot of them were designed by a guy from a company called Chameleon Lighting whose name was Colin. For the 'Bomber' tour, they had a huge lighting rig shaped like a bomber plane which would be lowered from the ceiling during the show, tilt as if it were taking a banking turn, and move out over the audience. For the 'Iron Fist' tour, the stage would be curtained before the show, then, at the start, the curtains would be drawn back to reveal a massive iron fist. The fingers would extend one by one, lights shining from each of the fingertips into the audience, then it would close up, move backwards and the set would begin, the music blasting from the speakers—only the stage would be empty. People would be looking round at each other, wondering what was going on, when the band would descend from the ceiling on a suspended stage which lowered onto the main stage.

For the 'Orgasmatron' tour, set design went further than it had ever gone before with the construction of a huge American-style locomotive—the Orgasmatron. The drum kit would be set on the platform at the rear of the train. The Orgasmatron had been the cause of a series of logistical nightmares throughout the UK leg of the tour. It needed its own truck to transport it and in some venues it wouldn't fit on the stage with the drum kit on the back. In the UK we'd been playing stadium venues. The American venues weren't so big. For some reason, no one had thought to check whether the Orgasmatron would fit inside them. It didn't. The damn thing stayed on its truck for the whole of the tour, carried the length and breadth of America. Totally ridiculous.

*

Between them, the guys got through a lot of drugs. There were two guys ex-SAS guys who used to supply them in the UK. They were the sort you wouldn't even think about messing with. Absolutely no fear of the law. From the way they went about things, it might not have existed. I can only suppose their experiences in service had given them a perspective from which the rule of law, to the extent that it registered at all, appeared only as foolishness, the consequences of falling afoul of it being nothing compared to the various hells they must have been through.

One night we were driving up into Scotland. We were to meet them just before the Scottish border. We were late and to occupy themselves while they waited for us, they'd lifted some massive speakers onto the roof of their saloon car, strapping them in place using cords running through the top of the windows along the ceiling. We turned up and proceeded in convoy down the motorway, the saloon car leading the way in the middle lane, crawling at 10 mph, the traffic building behind us, bagpipe music blaring out, over the motorway and across the hills, up into Scotland.

*

For the 'Iron Fist' tour, there was so much merchandise to transport we had to hire a three-and-a-half ton truck. There were three of us who took it in turns to drive. Joining us was a well-heeled woman engaged to a member of a the family who owned a major British supermarket chain (I won't say which). She didn't need to work and had come on the tour for a sort of hen party. She was only with us for a fortnight. She was extremely elegant, her hair elaborately coiffed, her speech effervescent as champagne. With her designer jeans and trainers (our uniform) she wore the largest emerald drop earrings. They looked completely incongruous. 'Are they real?' I asked her. 'Why of course, darling,' she replied.

I would ask to do the overnight drives, when the roads weren't so busy and there weren't so many distractions inside the truck. The band were playing four nights at the Hammersmith Odeon and I and the other merchandisers went back to a flat on the Portobello Road where we were to stay the night. We didn't think about the market being on and looked out of the window the next morning to see the truck surrounded by vehicles and shoppers. We couldn't hang around so we bundled into the truck and tried to ease our way out. We were reversing when we heard someone shout '*Whoa whoa whoa!*' before a slight jolt and the sound of bumper meeting bumper. We got down and had another look at the situation. We asked a stall owner if he wouldn't mind moving his stall. He did mind but he moved it anyway. We tried again, going backwards and forwards, working our way out by degrees, clunking and scraping and cursing. By the time we'd got the truck out into the road, we'd damaged three cars. Not having time to wait to locate the owners and take down insurance details, we scribbled the office's telephone number on some scraps of paper and stuck them under the windscreen wipers. Scattering apologies, we left the stall owner to rearrange his wares.

After London, we went on to Port Talbot, Crawley and Poole, from which we drove overnight to Portsmouth. This was the beginning of April 1982. It was 3 am, pitch dark. The eastbound road out of Portsmouth was closed, a convoy of police cars and military vehicles proceeding to the ports where warships were ready to set sail for the Falklands. It stretched for miles—this blazing train of cars and trucks, missiles and tanks borne on their backs, lumbering along the unlit road. It was without a doubt one of the most surreal things I have ever experienced, like something out of a movie. Really quite terrifying.

Stuck behind the convoy with no chance of overtaking and ready for something to eat, we decided to stop off at Exeter service station. The car park was packed with military vehicles. We had to drive around a while before we found a space to park up. We hadn't been travelling in convoy but I recognised one of our trucks and assumed that the tour bus wouldn't be far behind. We went inside and found it a sea of khaki—soldiers eating in the restaurant, drinking coffee, playing on the pinball machines—enjoying a poor meal and a bad cup of coffee before they went off to fight. To fight. It was a bizarre thought. It seemed like war was something we'd had done with, and here were all these troops. Some of them only looked about my age. Young, too young. It occurred to me that some of them might not return. It was in a daze that I walked further inside, through to the restaurant area. In our denim and leather, we stood out, and when the band turned up, they were quickly recognised and conversations struck up. Lemmy loved arcade games and was soon playing pinball and Space Invaders with some of the marksmen. They were joking that they should take him with them and were lining up to play against him, eager to take him down. We all got talking with the soldiers. We talked about the conflict but mostly we talked about other things—which is what I'm sure I would have wanted to talk about if I was just about to go and fight a war halfway across the world.

It was time for them to leave. We all struggled to think what to say, wished them all the best and tried not to show the anxiety we felt for them. Bizarre. It was totally bizarre. We were off to put on a rock show, while they were off to fight a war. It was awful watching them go, but then I thought it was some pleasant distraction for them to have spent a few hours hanging out with Motörhead, playing pinball with Lemmy. I won't ever forget them.

*

Once, when we were in Germany, we were travelling overnight to East Berlin. I was driving the Ford Granada estate. For company, I had Lemmy beside me. He was tired and wanted to get to the hotel. It would be quicker in the car than on the tour bus. In the back was the German promoter. It was quite unlike driving on an English motorway, the corridor so smooth and straight, a wire fence running alongside, towers and checkpoints strung along. There was a service station halfway, divided into two sections—one for West Germans, one for East Germans. Each population had its own entrances, shops, toilets. The latter were frequently used for illicit trade, goods slid under the gaps between the cubicle walls and the floor. We'd bring consignments of Levi jeans, Adidas trainers— goods that weren't available to East Germans. These would be pushed through to the cubicle occupied by an East German trucker in exchange for Russian vodka.

Cash was essential for passage down the corridor. Vehicles were scrutinised by the roadside police. If you were spotted with foreign license plates, you were pulled over and fined. No matter what, you paid. With the spotlights, the guns and the dogs, you didn't need much persuading. We were guaranteed to be stopped, I knew. The front light was on inside the car so that Lemmy could read his book—a history of the SS, a swastika stark on the cover—throwing into relief the dense cloud of cigarette smoke that had accumulated. Through the haze, I made out a policeman flagging us down. I pulled up. Lemmy wound down his window. I was surprised to see that the night air was clear; Lemmy's chainsmoking had made me think it was a pea-souper. The guard took a long hostile look at Lemmy, taking in the SS history, the rings on his fingers, the leather jacket ornamented with badges and the German helmet on his head.

'Alright?' said Lemmy, as only Lemmy could.

The officer looked ready to spit, meanwhile the German promoter leaned forward to try and placate him. Though I could speak German, I was quite happy to leave it to him. Pete Gill, who was the drummer for Motörhead for a couple of tours and who had played previously with The Glitter Band, used to drive with me quite a bit in Germany and he also spoke the language. We didn't get much chance to exercise our fluency, however, since the Germans invariably spoke better English than we spoke German. (We used to joke that if you wanted to know how to spell an English word, ask a German.) The guard told us how many marks we needed to pay, we amassed the sum and Lemmy handed it over.

'There y'are,' he said.

The officer said nothing, only flicked his head for us to be on on our way, his narrowed eyes looking as if they never wanted to settle on Lemmy again. It was typical of him, fooling around like that. Pure insouciance. We were stopped at least five times and parted with at least £6,000.

Leaving Berlin, I was on my own. Before getting on to the autobahn, I had to go through passport control. The station consisted of a shed. Alone, no one else around, the sense of isolation was profound. I was given back my passport and sighed my way on to the autobahn. As I was cruising along, three black limousines with tinted windows drew alongside. One of the windows rolled down and a black-clad man with black sunglasses stared out at me. I gripped the steering wheel and tried not to show my terror. The window rolled up and the limousines overtook me. I sighed some more, desperate to get where I was going, thinking I would rather have had Lemmy with me after all.

Motörhead's tour bus would nearly always be subject to close inspection when passing a border. According to regulations, however, guards were permitted only in the front part of the bus. The tour manager would collect everyone's passports early in the evening to be able to present them without having to go waking everyone up and asking for them. Knowing the band and their reputation, the bus would nearly always be asked to drive over to one of the buildings to be searched. Sniffer dogs would be brought out, mirrors used to check underneath the bus. Sometimes we would be travelling on the same road in and out of a town. On these occasions, to avoid trouble at checkpoints, we would bury any illicit goods off the road in some sheltered (usually wooded) spot, noting precisely the locations (fifty steps perpendicular to the road from the Wild Animals Possible sign). These stashes could be left for days, even a couple of weeks. One time the drugs had been bagged up and someone was ready with the spade to get off and bury them when we realised that we had already reached the checkpoint. The bag was passed down to the back of the bus and stowed away.

Driving in convoy one night through West Germany we stopped off at a service station. It was cold and we were hungry. When we left the station we found it had started snowing while we'd been in the restaurant. Heavily. There was a foot-deep carpet of snow. We had an eighteen-hour drive ahead of us—eighteen hours in normal conditions. Thankfully we had the next day off, so there was no hurry. We set off, the trucks leading the way.

We hadn't gone far when the lead truck skidded, the cab swinging off the road. The driver was able to climb down, unhurt. The autobahn was closed off so it could be cleared. The snow ploughs, however, quite uncharacteristically for the congenitally efficient Germans, were delayed. We were told by the traffic officer that we would have to get off the autobahn, it was unsafe to travel. We knew it was unsafe to travel but we had to be on our way, we hadn't time to stop. The traffic officer told us he was sorry, he could not permit us to travel in such conditions. He said that a car would escort us off the autobahn and to a hotel where we could stay the night and continue our journey in the morning, provided the roads had been cleared sufficiently. We thanked him for the offer of assistance but we explained that, while we understood the risks, we *had* to get on, we would be careful, could he let us? He was wavering, we could see. In the end we persuaded him to let us continue on our way and one of the bus drivers told me how to drive in snow. 'Don't grip the wheel, just go with the flow. If the car goes one way, let it. If it goes another, don't try and bring it round. Just follow the car. The more relaxed you are the better. In fact, you're probably best off drunk.' The truck was pulled back onto the road and off we went, weaving our way at 60 mph along the endless white stretch, deserted but for our intrepid convoy.

4

Me in the making

I was always afraid of Motörhead—bearded, loud, leather-jacketed. Spinal Tap had nothing on them for sheer craziness. The decade I spent with them was the most arduous, infuriating and nerve-racking of my career, but it was also without a doubt the most fun. At the end of it I had the greatest proof of my capacity to take a rock band on the road: if I could handle Motörhead, I could handle anyone. One thing they weren't was boring.

*

When I first went on the road with the guys I was filled with apprehension. That first day I had walked into the offices at Great Western Road and seen Lemmy and Fast Eddie talking to Motorcycle Irene, I had been struck by the bristling facial hair, the denim and the leather. Their crew looked just as intimidating. I was relieved to find, however, that they were almost all at least fairly pleasant—to me, anyway. Their tough exteriors weren't entirely misleading, though. I heard that one of the drivers ended up imprisoned in India for murder.

The first time I travelled on the tour bus was at the end of a tour of Europe. It was decided that there was no need to have two merchandisers, nor was the merchandising van needed, and so Janet was to drive the van, in which I had been travelling up to that point, back to England, meanwhile I would carry on with the rest of the tour and be given a bunk on the bus. I hadn't received this last piece of information, however, and so, having boarded the bus, I looked around for a place to kip. There were two empty seats at the back, so I curled up in the corner and watched the guys stomping up and down the bus, drinking cans of Special Brew and bottles of vodka, before dozing off. My head lolling, I lifted leadened eyelids to see Lemmy fiddling with the television. I didn't know what time it was or how long I'd been dozing. He looked round at me. 'Well if you're up you might as well watch this with me,' he said.

I blinked and looked at the video cassette he had in his hand. *Excalibur*. I hadn't seen it. He stuck the cassette in the player. This was start of my staying up watching films with him. Or rather, of my watching the films while he went off and did something else. He would always ask for a review after the film had finished. If I'd known this that first night, I'd have watched it more closely. The credits were rolling when he came back and asked me what I thought of it. I obliged, my thoughts few and not well-articulated. He didn't seem to mind, though, nodding approvingly when I finished. He put his hands on his knees and stood up. 'Do you know where your bunk is?' he asked. 'No,' I said. I didn't say I didn't know I had one. He showed me where it was, I said goodnight and climbed into it. From behind my curtain, I could hear him walking up and down the bus in his heavy boots, the crack and fizz as he opened another can of Special Brew. Exhausted, I fell asleep.

I was glad I'd stayed up and watched the film that night. Though I liked my sleep and was by no means a cinephile, a friendship had been established. For all that he might have given the contrary impression, Lemmy was no lout. He was incredibly intelligent and very well-read. His father had been a vicar, as had my step-father. He abhorred the mistreatment of women. Though it was always assumed young girls would be parading through his hotel room, I always used to imagine he spent his free time watching movies and making Airfix models. I hadn't known him long when I showed up at his flat one morning to drop something off from the office. He answered the door in his dressing gown and invited me in. On the dining table I saw that he was in the middle of assembling a Spitfire. It was quite an eye-opener.

I didn't get on so well with the other band members, Phil 'Philthy Animal' Taylor and Fast Eddie. I didn't speak much with Phil. Early on I had a sense of hostility, which I put down to his sister's being in charge of Motörhead's official fan club. She followed the tour with her boyfriend and they would sell the fan club's T-shirts at the gigs. When Eve Carr found out about this, she went ballistic. It was thus a little awkward between us, the merchandisers, who worked for Eve, and them. Phil being her brother, he sided with her. There was no real antipathy, we just didn't get on. I think it was really down to our simply not having much in common.

With Fast Eddie things were rather more awkward. One of my friends, an American girl called Vanessa, came to a gig at Birmingham Odeon. The band were staying at a hotel opposite. After the gig we went up to a bar on the top floor. My friend, smiling, talkative and gregarious, tended to attract attention, and when Eddie came up, he was quick to introduce himself. He hadn't finished his first drink (not his first of the evening) and I could see that he was about to pounce. Casually, I took Vanessa to one side and warned her that he was going to try one on her. I went to get another drink and Vanessa returned to the table. I went back to the window ledge I had been sat on, next to one of the roadies, a Liverpudlian called Paul, with whom I got on very well. This proved to be an unfortunate choice of seating.

Out of the corner of my eye, I saw Fast Eddie jump out of his chair. He daggered me with his eyes. 'Fucking bitch,' he said. Uh-oh, I thought. He stalked over, pushing chairs out of his way. 'Who the hell do you think you are?' I cast a look round the bar and saw that Vanessa had disappeared. Paul told him to take it easy. Eddie ignored him. He pushed me backwards and dragged me across the ledge by my leg. It flashed through my mind that he was going to dangle me from the window. I tried to kick me leg free, lashing out with my other foot. 'Fucking cow,' he said. He lifted my leg and then dropped it. I heard Paul shouting at him and I wriggled away from the window. Looking round, I saw Paul, his fist red, dragging

Fast Eddie away. 'Go to bed,' he told him. Eddie slunk off, effing as he went.

Needless to say, I was pretty shook up by the incident. I went to bed and didn't count up the merchandise as I normally did. The next day I got a call from the office asking for the stock details. I told them I hadn't done it—any of it—counted the merchandising money, done the spreadsheets to fax over, nor taken a stock count. Why not? I was asked. I told them what had happened with Eddie. Doug was informed and I had another call a short while after from him telling me that I could expect an apology from Eddie later that day. Sure enough, that afternoon, Eddie came over. 'I think it's best if we keep out of each other's way,' he said. Not quite an apology but I wasn't going to press him for one. He called me a snitch. I denied the accusation. He said I *was* a snitch. I wasn't prepared to argue, thinking this was the sort of interchange you'd expect from the school playground. After that, we only ever nodded to each other; we never spoke. Paul used to joke about the incident. If he ever needed anything—10p for the phone, say, or a cigarette lighter—he used to pick me up and shake it out of my pockets. The last I knew he was working for Cliff Richard and the Shadows. The change of employer had necessitated a change of image, the first part of which was a haircut.

*

This wasn't the only instance of rough treatment that went on while I was with Motörhead. The band were playing the Hammersmith Odeon at the start of a horrifically long tour. We were setting up behind the fortified merchandising stall which stood five feet from the floor and had been erected by the merchandising company to deal with the crushes of boisterous customers, when four Hells Angels came up and chucked a bag over the top. 'You're selling these,' they said. We looked in the bag and found a load of Hells Angels T-shirts. Looking down at the beards and the hands ringed as if knuckledustered, we didn't object. We only sold a couple.

It was just as well we didn't make a fuss. Later that night, while the band was playing, the tour manager's girlfriend had gone backstage to have a sleep in the dressing room. While she was lying on the couch, a couple of Hells Angels walked in. She asked them what they were doing. They said they were getting a drink. She told them they weren't allowed backstage. They ignored her. She told them to get lost. Taking exception to this, they threw her downstairs. She was rushed off to hospital. It was thought she might have broken bones.

This wasn't the only run-in with the Hells Angels. They were always showing up to Motörhead gigs. I learnt how not to antagonise them—by staying out of their way, and if they asked you to do something that wouldn't overly endanger yourself or others, to just do it.

We were in Norfolk one time and one of the Trasnam truck drivers we hired invited us to a party that was going on down the road. A great bear of a man who looked rather like a young Father Christmas (though scarier if you didn't known him), we used to call him Motörhead Ted for the simple reason that he drove with us and was called Ted. (The other Transam driver was nicknamed 'Pigpen' on account of the state of his cab, which, like himself, he didn't clean once during the entire course of a tour.) It was a day-off, so we all traipsed off to a remote farmhouse where the party was being held, a fleet of motorbikes standing outside. Though this was a big clue, we didn't pick up on the fact that it was a Hells Angels party until we walked in and saw all the beards and emblazoned waistcoats. When I realised that I was the only woman, my sense of unease increased. The other guys were uneasy too. Whispering together, we decided that, for my safety, I would be introduced as Lemmy's girlfriend. We didn't stay long, and I left unscathed.

It was only when I went to Copenhagen that I learnt of the cultural diversity amongst the Hells Angels. A few of the club's Danish representatives were hanging out in Motörhead's dressing room before a show. I had noted the solid gold jewellery they wore, having only ever known the UK members I'd come across to wear silver. As well as being more affluent, these Hells Angels were much more polite, 'please' and 'thank you' in their vocabulary. They looked to Lemmy before asking if I wanted any of their drugs. Lemmy said, 'Of course you can offer her; she's one of us.' I had never been offered drugs by a Hells Angels before. Don't mind if I do, I said, as much for the novelty as wanting a kick.

Having mentioned motorbikes, I might mention here that Lemmy absolutely hated them. For the video 'Killed by Death' there's a part where Lemmy is riding one while being caressed by a blonde riding pillion. When they were filming there was no chance of Lemmy actually riding one, so the motorbike was mounted on the back of a truck so that all Lemmy had to do was sit on it.

Another of Motörhead's films—one of their earliest—was 'Eat the Rich'. A small theatre was hired to screen the film over a couple of days, which was all very exciting. After the premiere we went on to a nightclub managed by Würzel's girlfriend for a champagne celebration. I remember that as being a really great night.

*

Perhaps the worst ever venue Motörhead played was in Holland. The Dutch promoter was paying us in cash. When we arrived at the venue, we were sure we must have made some mistake: it was a cowshed—an unconverted cowshed. There were cows in the fields surrounding and when we ventured inside we found straw on the floor, not particularly fresh. The merchandise stall was pointed out to us. It was a feeding pen. Despite the utter unsuitability of the venue, Motörhead were loathe to disappoint their fans. So they played the cowshed—to a sell-out crowd.

Afterwards, when it was time to talk money, I went out to a small outbuilding to look for the promoter. Inside, I found two Hells Angels talking to a third man I didn't know. As my eyes adjusted to the gloom, I saw that each of the Hells Angels was pointing something at the guy, and, my vision sharpening, that what they were pointing at him were guns. (This wasn't the first time I'd seen a gun, one of Motörhead's truck drivers having smuggled guns into the UK from Europe by taking advantage of the selective inspections made by customs officers.) Just why they were pointing them at him, I didn't know. The guy looked like he knew how to handle himself and didn't seem especially perturbed. I decided to leave them to it and go back later.

One time, in Austria, Motörhead had played another unsuitable venue. A tent had been erected in a car park, two feet of snow on the ground. This wouldn't have been so bad if there hadn't been two feet of snow *inside* the tent too. The show was very nearly cancelled but, thanks to a team of guys shovelling all day, the snow was sufficiently cleared for it to go ahead.

One gig in Reading had to be cut short after a squad of undercover drugs police circulating amongst the audience started making arrests. It wasn't long before things started to kick off. By the end of the show, the audience was seething, the atmosphere crackling with aggression. As soon as the band finished the set, they got off the stage and, without playing an encore, everything was packed up pronto and we hurried out into the car park, a police car escorting us out of town.

Though there was nothing like modern health-and-safety regulations in place then, I remember one time when a fire officer came to inspect the stage set and wasn't satisfied that the backdrop was sufficiently fire-retardant. 'Bollocks,' said Lemmy. 'Let me see your certificate.' The fire officer said he didn't have his certificate with him. 'Well then,' said Lemmy. The officer said the backdrop was a hazard and could not be used. 'What do you mean I can't use my fucking backdrop?' said Lemmy. 'You can't use the backdrop,' said the officer. Lemmy gave him a long hard stare then said, 'Let me show you something.' Taking his Zippo lighter out of his pocket, he flicked a flame and held it against the backdrop. Anticipating a whoosh of fire, I was relieved to see that nothing happened. 'There,' said Lemmy, snapping the lid closed. 'That good enough for you?'

This wasn't the only controversy that the backdrop caused. In the middle near the bottom, just a few inches tall, was a swastika. This had attracted not a little protest. How anyone had spotted it, I don't know. Lemmy (a Word War II whizz and no Nazi) responded in his usual brusque manner. '*That* is not a Nazi swastika,' he said. 'The Nazi swastika is a left-right reversal of that symbol, which so happens to represent Kali, Hindu goddess of death.'

There were plenty other hazards, though, apart from the backdrop. The night after the Reading gig we were in Cambridge. Shortly before the gig there was a huge explosion. My then second husband was the lighting designer. In the hasty escape the night before, two of the explosives had been packed away primed. He had set the pyro on the stage and it had detonated, blasting his hand. The first thing we did was stick it under a cold tap. The skin was melted, running off his hand with the water. He was rushed to hospital where the wound was cleaned and dressed and—somehow!—he went on to the next gig.

The last night of another tour, in France, the band decided to use up all the explosives that were left over in a spectacular opening. It hadn't been the smoothest of tours. Phil Campbell had broken his leg and so had had to play his guitar from an armchair brought out onto the stage. The band struck their first chord.

BANG!!!

The building shook. Phil Campbell's armchair shot forward with the force of the explosion, coming to rest precipitously at the edge of the stage. The gels from the lights came unfixed and fluttered down to the stage like giant pieces of confetti. A couple of Marshall monitors were blown too. The stage wrecked, the crowd shaken, the band made a quick exit, one of the crew dashing onstage to wheel Phil Campbell off. Miraculously, we didn't get into any trouble. Some of us were jittery for a while afterwards, though. Phil could easily have ended up with another broken leg. Lemmy and Würzel found it hilarious.

Phil and Würzel had joined the band after Eddie Clarke left. I got on with both of them much better than I had got on with Eddie. Würzel was delightful. He looked completely wild, hence his nickname, derived from Worzel Gummidge, which he had been given while he was serving in the British Army. When he opened his mouth, a refined southern accent came out, his speech liberally sprinkled with 'please's and 'thank you's and 'Would it be too much trouble...?'s. In his denim and leather, the only giveaway that he wasn't as rough as he looked was the Rolex he wore on his wrist.

One summer the band had a gig at Le Mans. They were to fly in, while the crew was to go on the tour bus. It was only going to be a short stay—in, play the gig, and out—and so we were to sleep on the bus rather than go to a hotel. The noise was horrendous, the cars snarling and screeching incessantly as they tore round the circuit. I'd been asked, if I could, to sell T-shirts at the gig. I couldn't on account of the place being absolutely rammed. I ended up running errands instead, going out to buy food, the nearest outlets a thirty-minute walk in the noise and the glare and the heat, the food cold by the time I got back.

*

Motörhead were always getting into trouble. In the end, they achieved such notoriety that they were barred from hotels the world over. I always thought it was crazy that this should have happened. They were never known to trash anything, they were never nasty or ever hurt anyone. It was all an image thing. While potential guests may have been put off staying at a hotel if they knew Motörhead were staying there too, I'm sure the hotel wouldn't have lost out. The bar probably made more money during one of their stays than it did in a regular month.

The well-known rock journalist Kris Needs toured with Motörhead for a while writing a piece for Time Out magazine and gathering material for a book (sadly unrealised) on the band. He cut a striking and not entirely respectable figure with his jet black punk hair. I got to know him quite well and one night we went out to a nightclub. Our photo was taken. I thought nothing of it until it appeared the next morning in the pages of the *News of the World*. My first thought was, what would my mum think? Thankfully, she didn't see it.

One night, at a gig in Birmingham, when the Falklands War was underway, Kris turned up in a T-shirt emblazoned with the words 'FUCK ARGENTINA' which he'd bought from one of the bootleggers outside the venue. The band said they wanted to wear those T-shirts onstage that night, so Kris was sent back out to go and buy fifty for them and the crew. This was the one night the guys appeared wearing bootlegged T-shirts.

The band's notoriety did have its upsides, though. On one Emirates flight we had just reached cruising altitude and the drinks trolley was promptly wheeled down the aisle. The stewardess asked the nearest band member if they would like a drink. 'Jack Daniels and coke,' he said. The stewardess reached under the trolley, brought out a box of twenty-four Jack Daniels miniatures and set it down in front of him, along with a single can of coke. 'And for you?' she said to the next. This went on, each served with a box of whatever spirits they wanted and a single can of mixer. Presumably it had been decided that the band would be less likely to cause trouble if they were plied with drink and sent into a stupor. The stewardess came to me and I asked for champagne. She set down a single bottle. Dejected, I reckoned she must have thought I wasn't with the band. She was duly corrected, however, by one of the crew, and returned, apologetic, with a half-dozen box of champagne miniatures for me. Given how some of them could be when they'd had a few, this wasn't a risk-free strategy, but as far as I remember, the flight passed without event.

Bad as some of Motörhead's behaviour was, a lot of it was staving off boredom rather than wanton destructiveness. Most of their misbehaviour was purely prankish. One of Lemmy's favourite hotel pastimes was messing around with signs. At one hotel in Sheffield there was a board with a notice written in magnetic letters. These he rearranged to make a new notice unappreciated by the hotel staff. At another hotel in Newcastle, after a show one night as we were leaving the hotel bar, we moved the signs put out to direct guests to breakfast in the dining room the next morning, directing them instead to the ballroom. We moved the tables and chairs too. The next morning we looked through and saw guests seated round the tables looking hungry. Eventually, someone came out and asked one of the hotel staff when they could expect breakfast to be served. But breakfast *was* being served, said the steward, as it was every morning in the dining room between 7 and 10 am. Several groups bustled into the dining room a few minutes later, just in time to catch the eggs and bacon before service stopped.

Some hotels we didn't want to go back to even if they would have had us. One of these was the Presidential Hotel in Athens. We went up in the lift to the rooftop bar one night and found that it was closed. We all got back in the lift and, before anyone had pressed a button, it began to descend slowly. The doors remained open and we could see the floors going past. After about three floors, the lift started to plummet, the numbers on the back of the lift doors on each floor whizzing by—18, 17, 16... Seeing two of the other guys exchanging a glance of wild terror, I thought with perfect clarity that that was it, my time had come, I was going to die. I clutched the handrails and braced for the impact.

We hit the basement floor with a jolt, falling forwards and backwards, against the mirrored panels and into each other. To our surprise, the lift bounced back up and came to rest halfway up to the ground floor. Our eyes met as we confirmed for each other that we hadn't just died, then we began to climb up out of the lift into the lobby. Various of the hotel staff rushed forward to help us up, one of them remarking that the lift was prone to such malfunctions, had been for some time. Several people obviously in need of medical attention, the rest of us not so obviously, an ambulance was called. Paramedics duly appeared. One of them asked how I was. I said my back was hurting. I was told I should get into an ambulance with two other guys who had sustained back injuries and had to be wheeled out of the lobby in wheelchairs. I climbed up into the ambulance, the door slammed shut and we lurched off at a lick. Not only had the wheelchairs not been strapped in, their brakes hadn't been applied. The siren bell ringing, we hurtled along, tipping into the corners, swaying as we switched lanes, the wheelchairs rolling backwards and forwards, slamming into the walls, the guys scrabbling for something to hold on to while I tried to grab hold of their chairs. It was like something out of a sixties slapstick film.

Having arrived at the hospital in slightly worse condition than we left the hotel, we were taken through to the casualty ward. The guys were seen to ahead of me, their injuries being the worse. Eventually I was asked through to a room where the doctor proceeded to wash his hands in the filthiest basin of water I've ever seen. The water was grey and opaque. He asked me to lie down on the bed, the paper covering not having been changed since the previous patient had lain on it and still smeared with their—or perhaps an even earlier patient's—blood. I told the doctor I was sure I would be fine, apologised for wasting his time and hurried out, wincing, a hand on my lower back. I went back to the hotel and up to my room, taking the stairs this time. I woke the next morning with a stiff neck and back. Uncomfortable as I was, I was sure it was nothing that warranted putting myself in that doctor's filthy hands.

I remember one time we were on tour in Scandinavia. It was midsummer and the sun, though low on the horizon, hadn't set. To get to the next venue we had to catch a ferry across a fjord. We arrived at the ferry terminal early in the morning, well before the ferry was due to sail so we pulled in at a lay-by beside a lake. We got off the bus and went for a walk round the lake. We came to a large house, a little way along the shore from which was a jetty to which a rowing boat was moored. Seeing no lights in the windows of the house, we thought its occupants must be asleep and so decided to borrow the boat. We climbed in and quickly climbed out when it started to sink. Within minutes, the boat had disappeared, a few bubbles coming to the surface. We all felt really bad. Würzel, looking to make recompense, decided to mow the owner's lawn using the ride-on lawnmower that was sitting on the grass. Firing the engine, he familiarised himself with the controls, then set about it. A light switched on in the house. Würzel, oblivious, carried on mowing while we waited for the owner to come bounding out. The light, however, went off. No doubt the householder had looked outside, seen the gang of wild-looking men and decided to stay put. The bus driver, a man called Maurice, went after the lawnmower, raking up the grass and putting it into piles, doing a neat job until his foot was bitten by a swarm of mosquitoes, after which, with much buggering, he hobbled over to a garden chair to inspect the wound.

Würzel finished mowing the lawn and we went back to the bus. By this time, however, the driver's foot had swollen to such an extent that he couldn't get his boots on and was in such pain that he couldn't push the pedals. Having no time to lose, we set off, he steering, while a couple of us used poles to operate the pedals. 'Clutch!' he'd shout. Then: 'Break!' We crawled along the shore at just over walking pace, reaching the terminal, again, too late, the ferry sailing out when we arrived.

Moored at the jetty, however, was a speedboat. Someone suggested we try and hire it. We went over, found the owner and asked him if he'd be willing to take us across the fjord. He said he would, for a fee. We agreed on the amount and climbed aboard, me, my fellow merchandiser Jan and the band. The bus would be driven to our hotel, Maurice now able to drive again having managed to soothe his feet with cold water. Before starting up the engine, the speedboat owner switched on a stereo system and Frankie Goes to Hollywood came blasting out. Crossing the fjord on that crystalline morning, my face whipped by wind and spray, 'Relax' in my ears above the roar of the engine, I remember thinking this will make a memory that will be hard to forget—as proved to be the case. We reached the other side and a police escort met us to take us to the venue. Evidently not having any patrol cars available, we bundled into a couple of mobile police cells. Considering the antics of the morning (trespassing, destruction of property, disturbing the peace), this was perhaps not an inappropriate choice of vehicle.

To be fair, however, given some of the behaviour I witnessed in Scandinavia, we hadn't done anything too atrocious—at least by the standards of the season. The impression I'd got from the time I'd spent in those northern countries was that in the darkness of the year, when the sun barely comes up, the people go into a sort of hibernation. Then, come the light, they make up for all the life they've missed.

We were in Finland, again in midsummer. The sun shone all day and our hotel, all glass, was like a greenhouse. I had to run a cold bath to sleep in. It seemed that the Finns didn't have to worry about sleep: they were in the bar all night, partying like mad. One night we were down there and one guy (long-haired, big-bearded) got into an argument with his girlfriend. In an access of drunken rage, he grabbed her hair and banged her head on the table, then dragged her limp body off with him. I couldn't believe it; it was what you'd expect of the Vikings. I called the receptionist over. From her reaction, it seemed that this was all pretty usual.

*

One of the ways the guys used to entertain themselves on tour was by playing competitions of various sorts. I remember we held a chess tournament once. Lemmy, who loved chess, said he wanted to watch me and Phil Campbell play each other. We both thought we were very good. Lemmy watched us for about five minutes then burst out laughing. 'I'll only entertain the possibility of sitting down to play either of you after you've had a *lot* more practice.' He went off and we carried on playing with reduced enthusiasm.

Other games weren't so civilised. As you might expect, Motörhead's idea of fun was a little more hazardous than most people's. One of their favourite pastimes was a game of their own invention called 'The Dance of the Flaming Arseholes'. This would normally be played with up to three people; any more and it became a little *too* dangerous. The game had to be played in quite a large space—an auditorium, say, or a sizeable backstage dressing room. The rules were as follows: each person had a toilet roll, stood on a table, dropped their trousers and unravelled the roll, keeping hold of the end. This was then inserted between the buttocks and the other end of the roll was set alight. There would be shrieks and yelps as the flames got closer. (As you might imagine, toilet paper goes up *very* quickly.) The winner of the game was the player who left the toilet roll in place. As the only female around, it wasn't a game I ever joined in, nor one I wanted to spectate. The guys used to get quite embarrassed if I was around. In one form of the game, the toilet roll was laid round a corner so that I couldn't see the guys on the table while they were unaware of how close the flames were getting. I don't think the winner of a game was ever determined, such was the general hysteria into which everyone was thrown and which made no clear judgement possible. Thankfully, the band were quite adept and the doctors were never called for.

Another competition we played was to see who could stay awake the longest. On one tour—dubbed the 'No Sleep At All' tour—one crew member lasted eleven days. Lemmy always used to say that after the first three days without sleep, you're over it. By the fourth day, I could see what he meant, but I didn't see the point in staying awake any longer and knew that it mustn't be healthy. I found that I functioned best on six hours of sleep. I'd heard that Margaret Thatcher used to manage on four. Busy as I was, I doubted I was as busy as her and decided I could afford the extra couple of hours.

For the amount he slept, Lemmy might have been playing a no-sleep competition all the ten years I was with him. He was one of those people who love to burn the candle at both ends. Everyone said he would die on stage. He was always taking speed, never without a bag of it. He'd dip in the blade of his flick knife and sniff it up off the tip, or else use his fingernail. We thought it had become essential to his functioning; if he stopped taking it, he'd simply keel over. Alcohol was another essential, vodka his favourite drink before he switched to Jack Daniel's. He never touched heroine. It was said that his detestation of the drug was due to his losing the love of his life to it. If he found any member of the crew using it, they would be fired immediately.

Lemmy wasn't the only one to take speed. We all did. It was part of our routine. Before every gig, after we'd had something to eat, we'd go to 'the Surgery'. This was a flight case with a large mirrored top that would be wheeled out onto the left corner of the stage, every night, on top of which a line of speed would be cut for every member of the band and crew. Every evening the same: finish setting up, have something to eat, go to Surgery, and the night would begin with the doors opening and the house music played through the PA.

Bad as this communal drugs-taking might have been, I'd seen worse. And no, I'm not talking about another heavy metal band; I'm talking about a celebrated orchestra. Before the show, the musicians took their seats and a large bag of coke appeared at the end of one row, the mouth of which was sealed but for a small gap in which a straw had been inserted. The holder of the bag stuck the straw up his nose, took a sniff and passed it to his neighbour, who did the same (with the same straw!). I watched as the bag went along, through the brass section, up into the percussion section. I was astonished.

After one tour, we were in Calais to catch a ferry back to England. Going through customs, we were asked to get off the bus so that an inspection could be made. The drivers always liked me to stay on board with them during inspections, the idea being that a female presence would confer an air of respectability on the bus. On this occasion, however, I had a gram of coke on me, which I had completely forgotten about having secreted it in the turn-up of a jean-leg. Sniffer dogs were brought on. When one of them thrust its nose down to my trainers I almost fainted. The dog sniffed, sniffed again, then went on. I made an effort not to show my relief. The only reason I can think that the dog made no fuss over me was that the smell of some weighing scales down the back of the sofa was stronger. The driver denied any knowledge of the scales when they were pulled out. There was no chance of their finding any of our fingerprints on it; we hadn't touched it. He told me later that it must have been there for about a year or so. We got through customs and boarded the ferry, arriving safely home. Five days later we heard the news of the Zeebrugge ferry disaster, in which 193 of those on board the MS Herald of Free Enterprise lost their lives after it capsized due to one of the doors having been left open and water flooding the car deck. It could so easily have been us. As I write this my thoughts are with those who passed, may they rest in peace. Those of us who escape such tragedies can only wonder, and go on.

The most coke we ever did was in Brazil. In the UK you could expect to pay £60 per gram. In Brazil we found that you could get it for just £5 per gram—and it was a far superior product, the stuff you got in the UK having been cut with God only knows what. There, the stuff was pure as snow. Each crew member had about two or three grams on them at a time. Whole packets would be chopped up. It got to the point where people were saying they'd had enough, they didn't want any more. The purity of the product made for an altogether different kind of high, and it was one of these experiences unlike anything I'd had before that brought me to my renunciation of drugs.

One night, during our stay in Brazil, I'd gone up to my room, put my bags against the door and turned the TV on. *Cocktail*, starring Tom Cruise, was on in-house movies. I sat down to watch it. Lemmy, who was staying in the room across from mine, walked in and asked me what I was doing. I said I was watching the film. He said he was going to get something to eat and walked out. He came back later and asked me what I was doing. I said I was watching the film. 'It's the same film,' he said. 'I know,' I said, 'this is the third time I've seen it.' I turned my eyes back to the screen. 'I don't get it,' I said. 'I can't get my head round it, what's happening…' For all the close attention I'd given it, I was at a complete loss. Coming down later I was like a zombie. What brought home the danger of the drug was the thought: how can anyone not follow the plot of *Cocktail*? And so I gave up coke, and hardly touched another drug after that. I didn't like dope, or any other soporifics; I was always tired enough without taking them. Sometimes, so many times, you just wanted to curl up right where you were and sleep.

*

Food played a big part in the life of the band. This was surprising as no one ever seemed to eat that much. Partly this had to do with the drugs, partly it had to do with the variable quality of the catering. The worst we ever had it was in South America. Even in the five-star hotels we'd been told to keep our food refrigerated on account of cockroaches. One night I'd opened a packet of crisps and stuck it in the minibar fridge overnight, half-finished. When I opened the fridge the next day, the packet was moving. How anything managed to get inside the fridge, I've no idea. At a stadium venue, I passed completely on the food when I discovered that due to lack of kitchen facilities, the caterers had moved into the toilets and were mixing potato salad in the urinals.

Some of the caterers were more conscientious. I always felt sorry for two guys in Innsbruck who had just set up their catering company. We were their first customers. They had gone to extraordinary lengths, setting vases of flowers on the tables, arranging platters of dainty snacks, devising a traditional British menu. There was one problem, however: the food wasn't ready, and there's nothing worse than a bunch of guys who haven't had their drugs being told they have to wait for their food.

The one sure way of getting taken advantage of by the band was by showing weakness. If you did, you were ripped into unsparingly. The caterers came out shortly before the band were due to go onstage and apologised that the food wasn't ready. This didn't go down well. They promised that the food would be ready after the gig, lavishing apologies. Hungry, I decided to undertake a little exploration of the town and found a beautiful little café where I had a bite to eat.

The food still wasn't ready after the show. Some of the guys lost it completely. They went out into the car park and trashed the caterers' van, bashing it with heavy objects, slashing the tyres and throwing a tin of spaghetti hoops through the windscreen.

The most atrocious thing the band ever did was to a promoter's agent in Scandinavia. We spent six weeks touring Sweden and Norway. How anyone can spend that much time there is beyond me. Things were only made worse by the direness of the catering. Cream cheese. That was all there was to eat. A gastronomic Groundhog Day. It wasn't long before things kicked off. Cream cheese, cream cheese, nothing but cream fucking cheese, the band complained. The promoter's agent apologised but still the menu went unchanged. It was when we got to his hometown that the band decided to exact revenge. They handcuffed him to a flight case before the doors opened, stripped him of his clothes and covered him in cream cheese. Someone suggested they handcuff him to the 'Bomber', which they did, the promoter's agent yelling and shrieking the while. A lawsuit followed, only to be dropped after

Doug Smith carried out a swift negotiation. Not surprisingly, another promoter's agent was enlisted for the band's subsequent Scandinavian tours.

It's funny that such exception should have been taken to this catering quirk when I think the only thing I ever saw Lemmy eat was cheese. He absolutely loved cheese, any cheese, the smellier the better. If I ever remarked on the smelliness of a cheese he was munching on, Lemmy would tell me once you got past the smell, the taste was amazing. In the kitchen on the tour bus you'd always be able to find some cheese and crackers. I have the image of him stood in black socks, underpants and a T-shirt trying a variety of cream cheeses at the back of the bus etched indelibly in my memory.

Lemmy wasn't the only rock star I knew to have an addiction to cheese. Dave Brock of Hawkwind had an even bigger problem with it. Every night he would go into the dressing room where the food had been set out by the caterers and make straight for the cheese platters. He'd take the lot and stow it in a flight case dedicated to that special purpose. As the tour progressed, the flight case would fill up with cheese and at the end of it he would take it all home. Bear in mind that some tours lasted three or four months.

What state it must have been in when he got home I don't like to think. What made it so bad was that a number of the band and crew were vegetarians. Cheese was therefore one of the few things they could eat and there was never any around. However quickly you made for the dressing room, it was always gone. There weren't even any crackers. They'd always disappear too. There must be something about cheese and rock stars. Perhaps it's their tending to have addictive personalities. I heard somewhere that certain cheeses are meant to be as addictive as some Class A drugs.

The best cheese that I ever had was in Paris on a promo. We were doing an interview in a Michelin star restaurant and, being a vegetarian, there was nothing on the menu I could eat. They made me cheese on toast. But this wasn't just any cheese on toast. No, this was sort of a three-cheese soufflé, served on toast—*the* most incredible cheese on toast I've ever eaten.

For all the poor catering we endured, most of the time we ate very well. We could afford to eat at the best restaurants and order the best on the menu, though we did on occasion have trouble interpreting the foreign ones. In Italy, we'd gone for dinner at a restaurant, Würzel, Phil Campbell, Lemmy and me. Looking down the menu, struggling to find something I recognised, I saw '*scampi*'. 'Scampi!' I said. 'You know, I quite fancy scampi.' Phil and Würzel said scampi appealed to them too. So we ordered scampi. What duly arrived at our table, though, wasn't scampi—not what we knew as 'scampi' anyway—breaded and golden and served with chips. Instead what arrived was a great heap of crustaceans, which looked unnervingly alive, the thick pink-orange armour of their shells distinctly less appetising than a layer of golden breadcrumbs. I helped myself to more bread and balsamic olive oil dip. Meanwhile, Lemmy was tucking into a delicious-looking pizza. 'Pizza!' I said. 'I didn't see pizza on the menu! How did you get pizza?' He looked at me with bemusement. 'Pizza's pizza, isn' it,' he said. 'Wherever you are, you ask for pizza, you get fuckin' pizza.'

We found Italy held more than culinary surprises in store for us. I was astonished by the extent of the corruption. We arrived at a venue one night, the entrance down a side street filled with stalls. It looked like a market. As we made our way down the street we saw that all the stalls were selling bootlegged Motörhead merchandise. We contacted the local equivalent of Trading Standards, who turned up a short while later. I explained the problem. They nodded unsympathetically and told us we wouldn't be selling any merchandise that evening. Yes, we'd heard them right. Their wallets must have been bulging with backhanders. All that night the bootleggers sold their merchandise while we didn't sell a thing. I'd learnt a lesson.

In Genoa I went to collect a consignment of T-shirts from the airport. I was told that was not possible, I would have to go back in three days time. I said that was no good, I needed them then. I handed over a roll of lira and the problem disappeared. If you wanted something done, you only had to pay for it.

By the end of a tour I was always desperate for plain food. Beans on toast. When I got home that was the first meal I ate—with unsurpassed relish. In Paris, we'd gone for lunch at a restaurant on the Champs-Élysées. Craving something simple, I decided on egg and chips. It wasn't the fanciest of restaurants, not by any means. Self-service too. Yet the plate of egg and chips I made up for myself turned out to be the most expensive I've ever bought. With a bottle of red (nothing extravagant), the bill came to F1,320—about £120. That was another thing with Motörhead: no one ever shared a bottle of wine with a meal; everyone always ordered their own. It was the same with any other drink—vodka, whatever: we didn't use glasses, sometimes we'd use straws. No one ever said, 'Let's have a drink'; it was always: 'Let's drink.' One taxi-ride in Paris, a member of the crew had thrown up in the back. The driver stopped the car and told us to get out at once. Eventually, I managed to persuade him not to throw us out with a handful of francs.

*

The one regret I have from my time with Motörhead is that I was never invited onstage to sing 'We Are the Road Crew' with them. Every gig they would invite a member of the road crew to join them and sing the song with them. This wasn't so surprising, as some of the crew were famous in their own right. There was Dil, the monitoring engineer, who sported a handlebar moustache and a white boiler suit. On one occasion, in a Withnailesque moment of despair at not finding any booze, he drank a bottle of aftershave. Another was Hobsey, a sound engineer, who was responsible for the deafening levels and the longest-running member of Motörhead's crew. In a 1986 article in *Spin* magazine, Motörhead was pronounced the loudest band on earth with a record of 130 decibels—10 decibels higher than that recorded for one of The Who's concerts which had earned them the Guinness World Record for 'the world's loudest band'. I said to Lemmy once that I'd never been picked to go up onstage with them and asked him why that was. 'Our image wouldn't look too good if we invited you up with us,' he said. It wasn't just that I was a woman. Perhaps if I'd worn chunkier boots or a chain I might have been invited up. As it was, I didn't and wasn't.

Perhaps the strangest experience I had while I was with Motörhead was in Ghent. The venue the band were playing, Lemmy informed me, was once a Gestapo HQ. There was a palpable sense of evil which the lurid colours with which the walls had been painted to funk the place up failed to dispel. The lower floors contained cells, the smell of sewage fouling the air. After the gig I went to take a shower on the fourth floor. While I was in the shower block, I heard what sounded like a party going on next door, a big band playing, cheerful voices and laughter. It sounded like the ball from *The Shining*. When I went back down I said to the promoter it sounded like they were having a good time next door. He looked at me blankly. Next door? There was no next door. Still I could hear those bright brassy noises. No question. I checked for myself afterwards: as the promoter said, there wasn't a next door. I don't know how to explain what I heard, but hear it I did.

One of the most disappointing experiences during my time with the band was the one which I had been most excited about beforehand. We were in Switzerland and I had heard that David Bowie was backstage. Tingling with goosebumps, I went to ask Lemmy to introduce me. He rolled his eyes. I pleaded, begged. 'Come on then,' he said. We went through to the catering area. Lemmy opened the door. There was David Bowie, sat on a sofa. He looked up at us and got to his feet. 'David, this is Kim,' said Lemmy. 'Kim, David.'

I was mortified.

The first time I had seen him walking to his limousine in the car park of Preston Guild Hall I had been a teenager. The next time, he was up on the stage as the Thin White Duke, looking 10-foot tall in his waistcoat and flowing trousers. Standing before me now, he was as tall as I was. I was speechless. The superman was really a man. I'd heard about meeting your heroes but until then I'd always thought there must be exceptions and that he would be one of them. Thinking about it afterwards, however, I realised the fault was all mine.

Perhaps my best backstage memory was made *beneath* the stage of the Hammersmith Odeon (now the Hammersmith Apollo). Motörhead were playing and Brian Robertson from Thin Lizzy had joined them as a guitarist for the 'Another Perfect Day' tour. Phil Lyontt turned up, wearing a shocking pink sequinned suit. He looked *great*. He was backstage and he wanted to watch the show. I was going through to the foyer so he said he would come with me. I had to take him through a network of tunnels which ran under the stage. The lights were down and we hadn't ventured far before we were lost in the subterranean tangle. It took us half-an-hour to find our way back to the surface. There were grins and meaningful looks and remarks about what we'd got up to. The truth was, the only thing we'd got was lost. Neither of us said anything though. We decided to let them talk.

*

It was Christmastime in Paris that I had my first experience of tour-managing. We had the weekend off, which we were all delighted about. There was one gig left to play on the 23rd before we flew back to London on Christmas Eve. On the Saturday morning I got a phone call from the band telling me they wanted to be paid so they would have some spending money. Could I go and get the money accrued throughout the tour, in various currencies, changed into francs and pounds for them? I said I'd do my best. And so I spent my free Saturday before Christmas in Paris traipsing round all the bureau de changes. I don't know how I managed to get all the money changed but I did. I hauled the lot over to the hotel. When I went looking for the tour manager I found that he had disappeared. The last anyone had seen of him, it turned out, was just after the previous gig. Everyone had supposed he was in his room, sleeping. No one had any idea where he might have gone; he wasn't answering calls to the telephone numbers we had for him. I was asked to arrange the settlements for the show the previous night and see to everything for the last gig of the tour, which I did. We wrapped up on the 23rd and drove back to London for Christmas. I had shown that I could do the work of a tour manager, and so that's what I became.

I had an idea what I was letting myself in for but I hadn't realised just how consuming the new responsibilities would be. I began to see how the previous tour manager might have reached a point where he couldn't go on any longer. I was determined to stick to it though. With the new responsibility came a heightened profile. This was an extra thrill.

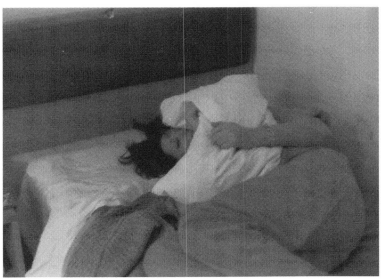

5

Birthdays and Other Bashes

I was in Vienna again, this time with Motörhead, staying in the same hotel as I had with Hawkwind after the accident at the traffic lights. It was a Sunday, a day off. (Motörhead always had Sundays off.) It was also the birthday of one of the crew. The concierge at the hotel had recommended a bar to one of the guys the night before, so we decided to go there to celebrate. We found the place—a rather plush-looking establishment with glass-topped tables and red velvet-upholstered chairs. There were several women hanging around wearing lots of makeup and not very many clothes, languidly sipping martinis. It was early in the evening and there weren't many customers. We sat down at a table and perused the drinks menus.

Glancing up, I saw a sharp-eyed member of staff heading for our table. I decided on an Old Fashioned and was about to ask him for it when he said something to one of the crew. I didn't catch what he said but it sounded like he was giving, rather than taking, orders. I saw puzzlement spread across the crew member's face before giving way to amusement. He looked at me, the employee doing likewise, though rather less amusedly. 'What is it?' I said. 'He says we have to go.' 'Go?' I said. 'Why?' I assumed we were being asked to leave because of what the guys were wearing. Though they *were* underdressed, I didn't think they deserved to be thrown out. The employee was adamant, however, and repeated something he'd just said, more insistently this time. He shot another sharp glance my way, which I didn't understand given that I was the smartest-dressed of the lot. I noticed some of the women looking over at our table and talking amongst themselves. 'Has anybody realised where we are?' twinkled the guy who was being addressed by the employee. I followed a long-legged woman as she clicked across the dancefloor, her jewellery and charged martini glass glinting in the light falling from the chandelier above it, to a table where a couple of women were sat, smoking, looking bored. It should have been perfectly obvious where we were. A brothel. The problem wasn't that we weren't dressed properly, it was that I was a woman. 'We're leaving,' we said, and quickly left.

This wasn't the first time I had been made to feel unwelcome by brothel-keepers in the company of Motörhead. We were in Hamburg and found ourselves in St Pauli, the city's red light district, one afternoon. The Beatles had played in a number of the clubs in the area when they were starting out. Ahead of us was the Reeperbahn—a stretch of seedy bars, strip clubs, sex shops and brothels. One particularly notorious street was the Herbertstraße, entry to which was forbidden to women. Lemmy had dared me to go down it.

'I don't think so,' I said.

'It's a dare.'

'I know it's a dare.'

'You could take my hat,' one of the crew suggested, offering his baseball cap.

'Yeah,' said Lemmy. 'Take his hat.'

And so there we were, at one end of the street. It was blocked off from the surrounding streets by high fencing. That it wasn't a place for women was made quite clear by the signs saying explicitly that women, along with under-18s, were 'VERBOTEN'.

'You want my hat?' said the guy with the baseball cap.

I looked at the fencing, goaded by the forbidding signs.

Lemmy wasn't with us. He'd be happy to hear about it all

afterwards. I took the cap.

'Pull up your collar too.'

I did so, stuck my hands in my pockets and went round the

fencing, wondering what I would find on the other side.

I looked down the street. There were rows of terraces either

side. They looked like shops, with large windows on the ground

floors. At a glance they might have been clothes shops with

mannequins on display. I could see, however, that these figures were

living. In most of the windows there was just one woman, in some of

them, two. They sat temptingly for the shoppers (exclusively male),

who could walk up and down the street, see what was on offer and

take their pick. I saw a guy take an appraising step back from a

window, purse his lips with decision, then approach the entrance, a

dour-looking madam taking him inside. The girl disappeared from

the window and was replaced by another. I was both intrigued and

disgusted. Looking around me, I was surprised by how clean the

street looked—just like the rest of the city—and in the daytime too.

Outside some of the establishments women were stood in groups, talking and smoking and laughing now and again, their eyes roving for customers. Anxious not to draw attention to myself, I hunched my shoulders, dipped my head, and carried on down the street. I was glad to have the other guys with me.

Ahead of us, outside another house, a big brassy woman was watching the street with densely mascaraed eyes. With her black shiny hair done up, her stout frame draped in garish silks and a feather boa round her neck, she looked like a pantomime dame. I was conscious that I was staring and lowered my eyes, only not before they met hers. I pulled the peak of the cap down and altered my bearings. Out of the corner of my eye, I saw her making her imperious way over. She said something in German. Keeping my head down, I attempted to look casually anywhere other than at the ill-tempered madam. '*Ay!*' she called to get my attention. Involuntarily, I looked up into her face. Her mouth dropped open and her arms went up. She started shrieking in German, flapping her arms, drawing the attention of other madams and their girls and their male customers. We moved on. 'Stay away from the windows!' one of the guys said, taking my arm, reminding me of what Lemmy had told me about buckets of water being thrown from the windows at unwelcome females. The woman's hollering was bringing more maquillaged madams out onto the street. Looking over my shoulder, I brought my head back round and narrowly avoided bumping into a sallow-faced man who mumbled something beerily in German. We carried on down the middle of the street, our eyes darting between the windows either side. A couple of unfriendly-looking women stepped out into the street, saying something to the bouncers outside an adjacent bar, gesticulating angrily. Just ahead of us, on the left-hand side, I saw a window flung open.

I broke into a run.

I didn't hear a splash but I heard plenty else going on behind me, muffled by the thudding in my ears, my rushing breath and pounding feet. I reached the end of the street and darted round the fencing, only slowing to a walking pace some distance further down the next street.

I looked around me, not knowing where I was. The other guys weren't with me; they must still have been down the Herbertstraße. The sleaze wasn't confined to that enclosed thoroughfare, though it was a little thinner, the erotic emporia interspersed with fast food outlets and dodgy discothèques, guys hanging about in doorways, singly or in groups. I could see other working ladies stood about, sauntering down the street, making display. It was only later that it occurred to me that, for all the ugliness of the brothels with their termagant keepers, at least the women there weren't plying their trade on their own, as they looked to be here. I wanted to get out of there. I pulled off the baseball cap and retraced my steps.

At least I could tell Lemmy I'd done the dare.

*

'I bet you won't jump out of a cake.'

This was another of Lemmy's dares. We were in Copenhagen and it was my second husband's birthday.

Wouldn't I?

I was in Würzel's hotel room with him and Phil Campbell, both of them having offered to help me make a 'cake' out of cardboard and tissue paper. Two tiers. I got into costume, crouched down and they lifted the cake on top of me, then covered it in shaving foam. A skirt of tissue paper would allow me to walk inside without my feet showing.

'How does it look?' I whispered.

'Delish,' said Phil.

When the cake was ready, Phil and Würzel carried it across to my husband's room. Other members of the band and crew were there with drinks and nibbles, music playing on a stereo. I crouched inside the cake, readying myself to spring out. The music stopped and the 'Happy Birthday' tune issued forth, everyone singing in raucous unison.

…Haaaaaappy Birthdaaaaaay toooooo yooooooouuuuuuu…

That was my cue.

I jumped out of the cake, flinging off the top in a shower of shaving foam.

'Happy Birthday!' I cried.

My husband almost spilt his Pilsner.

Würzel came forward with the bath robe I had told him to stand in readiness with and I wrapped myself up in it before climbing out of the destroyed cake. I noticed two roadies grimacing and swigging their beers desperately. 'They tried the shaving foam,' said Phil, scooping a fingertip and blowing it off. The room was a devastation of tissue paper and foam—on the floor, the walls, the ceiling—crisscrossed with streamers from a fusillade of party poppers. It was only a few moments before more shaving foam was being flung about the room, the stereo started playing again, the hotel room becoming a tumult of festivity. This made just another incident which contributed to the band's notoriety amongst hoteliers across Europe, though this was perhaps the only time they could have been said to trash anything.

Another of these incidents was at a hotel in Stratford-upon-Avon. It was just after Bonfire Night. Earlier in the day I had seen a box of fireworks reduced from £100 to £50. I bought them and took them back to the hotel with me. That evening, having a few drinks together in our hotel room, someone suggested that we set them off.

'Where?' someone said.

'There,' another said, pointing out of a window to the roof of the hotel entrance.

Helped by alcohol and drugs, we decided that this was a great idea, and proceeded to relocate to the roof, climbing out of windows, taking our drinks and the fireworks with us. Some of the guys started setting them up, others brought out chairs, and so there we were, on the roof, assembled for our fireworks party. The pyrotechnician took out a lighter and lit a rocket at the edge of the roof, darting back as it shot up into the air, streaming sparks.

BANG!

He ran forward again and lit another.

BANG!

A row of gerbs were lit next, multicoloured sparks jetting up, pouring over the edge of the roof.

'*Hey!*' came a voice from below.

When the sparks died down, the pyrotechnician went forward and peered over the edge of the roof.

'What's going on up there?'

A few of us went forward with our drinks. The doorman stood glaring up at us down on the car park. An oldish couple, presumably returned from dinner, got out of a taxi pulled up outside the entrance and craned their necks, aghast. The doorman shuffled backwards as we appeared at the roof edge, raising on his toes to see how many of us there were up there.

'Guests are not permitted on the roof!'

We made vague noises of surprise.

'Please go back inside at once!'

'Party pooper,' someone said.

We gathered up the unexploded fireworks and passed the chairs back through the window, then climbed back inside. One of the desk clerks was stood in the hallway looking stern and making reproofs tempered by the courtesy proper to hotel guests. The manager appeared and asked that we surrender the fireworks, which we did, on condition we could have them back when we left. Not because we wanted to use them but because of the principle of the thing. The manager waddled off, the desk clerk in tow, and we resumed our festivities more decorously.

*

The first birthday I celebrated on tour was with Uriah Heep, on their 10th anniversary tour. I was twenty. I hadn't told anyone and hoped no one would find out.

Somehow, someone did.

We were driving down the M4 to Wales. I was in the merchandise van, not driving this time. Jane said she needed the toilet, so we pulled off at a service station. To my surprise, the tour bus was there, along with the other trucks.

'What's going on?' I said.

'It's your birthday,' said Jane.

I groaned inwardly and climbed down from the van. This was also to be the first birthday party I'd ever had at a motorway service station, and it was actually really great. As well as booze, we had nibbles and music. Everyone sang 'Happy Birthday'. They sang it again later that evening when we got to the venue and sat down to dinner, after which I was presented with a massive bunch of flowers from the band and crew. It was exactly what I had hoped wouldn't happen, but I was so pleased that it did.

My thirtieth birthday I celebrated in Glasgow while I was on tour with Hawkwind. I was to meet my soon-to-be husband there, who was on tour with someone else. I got on the the train at Preston and settled into my seat. A short while later, a man walked past. He stopped. I'd never seen him before. He asked me if I'd like to have lunch with him. I smiled inwardly and thought, what the hell, why not? 'Alright,' I said, and followed him down the train to the first-class dining car. We had a good lunch and five or six gin-and-tonics. A very pleasant journey. As we disembarked at Glasgow, the man asked me for my number. He then asked me if I'd like to go with him to Japan. Thanking him, I said not. I didn't add that I'd just got engaged. I went on to my hotel and met up with Paul. In celebration, we ordered a bottle of Moët & Chandon. When we'd finished this, we ordered another. And another. By the day's end I'd drunk seventeen bottles, drinking myself sober three times in all. At the close of the day, I was sat in front of the television watching Frankie Howerd in a rerun of *Up Pompeii*—not a favourite show, but one I remembered watching as a girl, and which served to unleash a torrent of emotion: I was thirty, past it, my life about to end. Sleep eventually rescued me. Though I probably deserved to be, I wasn't sick at all.

It was some years later that I celebrated another, less momentous birthday on tour, this one with Concrete Blonde. We arrived at the venue in Atlanta run by Mark Parks, who I knew from when he had worked as a lighting designer for us. Cards had been delivered to the venue over the past week, several each day, some of them from the UK. He asked if it was my birthday. I told him it was but made him promise not to tell anyone else, they didn't know, and that was just how I wanted to keep it. I had enough on my plate besides embarrassment, and as the day went on things only got worse. Johnette's cat was travelling with her on the tour bus. I had gone to fetch something from it and, looking out of a window, saw two young fans (they were wearing Concrete Blonde T-shirts) playing with a cat that looked just like Johnette's. I darted out of the bus and over to them and asked them if that was their cat. 'We found him,' said one of the girls. 'He's a stray.'

If this *was* Johnette's cat...

I told them to wait there and not to let the cat out of their sight. I ran back to the bus and swept it to make sure that Johnette's cat wasn't on board. It wasn't. I ran back to the rescuers.

'That's Johnette's cat,' I panted.

'It *is*?' said the other girl. 'No way.'

'Yes way. Please could I have it?'

They handed the cat over. I clutched it to me, ignoring the nails scratching my top.

'Thank you, thank you,' I said. 'Johnette will be so so happy.' (She also wouldn't throw a fit.)

The girls were thrilled.

'Do you think you could tell her we found her cat?' said the first.

'Say, do ya think we could meet her?' said the second.

I said I thought that might not be possible, we had a lot to do. Which was true.

'How about after the show?'

'Maybe,' I said, thinking most certainly not. If Johnette found out that someone had let her cat off the bus, she'd go spare and none of us would hear the end of it, especially me. I thanked the girls again, and took the cat back to the bus, checked all the windows and left it with a biscuit.

Later that evening, everything and everyone ready, the audience seated, The Oblivious, who were supporting Concrete Blonde, went out. Holly Vincent, the lead singer, stepped up to the microphone and announced that the show would be starting a little differently that night. This was the first I'd heard. Concrete Blonde came out onstage too. A small knot tied in my stomach as I guessed what was about to happen.

A count in, a blast of guitars and a crash of drums, and the two bands launched into a punk rendition of 'Happy Birthday', punishing their instruments and their vocal chords. Apparently, according to Holly Vincent, that was what a girl from London would like. Never mind that I wasn't from London. I went up onstage at the behest of the band, accepted an extravagant bouquet, thanked the band and the applauding audience, and got off the stage as quickly as I could.

I hated being in the spotlight. That was one of the things which suited me about being a tour manager, where your work is done all in the background. (Being called Kim was great: since I didn't look like most people's idea of a Kim, I was able to go about less harassed than I might otherwise have been.) It was with distinct discomfort, therefore, that I turned up at a party thrown by Richard Branson in LA to find that there was a red carpet entrance for all the guests. Everybody who was anybody was there and the paparazzi had turned out in force. There are photographs of me making my red-faced way down the carpet, concealing myself behind my more gregarious companion's shoulders. More photographs were taken inside. It was a great party. Seal was the headline act. Just not my scene.

Perhaps the best birthday I ever celebrated during my time in the music business was my daughter Kennedy's. She was going to be four. I was working as a troubleshooter at the time on a six-day stint. I was to work the Monday till the Friday, missing the last night to travel home to be back in time for her birthday on the Sunday. There was no way I was going to miss it. My employers at EMI knew there were just two days in the year I absolutely wouldn't work: Kennedy's birthday and Christmas. It was at the beginning of the week that I got a call from a guy at EMI asking if I would work the Saturday. No, I said, I was going home on Saturday, it was my daughter's birthday, as I had made quite clear from the outset. When it was clear I wasn't going to budge, he asked me what I had planned for Kennedy. I said I didn't know. He asked me if Kennedy had ever been to Disneyland Paris. She hadn't. He told me that if I worked Saturday he would arrange for us to go to Disneyland for her birthday. How will that work? I said. Kennedy couldn't catch a plane by herself; I'd have to pay someone to take her. He said that could all be taken care of. Besides, I said, we'd have to set out on the Monday, after her birthday. Exciting as a trip to Disneyland would be, all I wanted was to go home.

Prima donna-ish, I started making further demands—not that I expected they would be met; rather, I thought this was the only way I would get them to drop it and allow me to go home for Kennedy's birthday. If we *were* to go, I said, I'd want for us to stay at one of the hotels at Disneyland inhabited by Disney characters. That wouldn't be a problem. And we couldn't go for just one night: we'd have to have at least three nights. That wouldn't be a problem either. But what about a cake? What sort of cake would she like? I'll need a car, I said, to take us from the airport—a limo. We could have a driver for the week. I should have known that this strategy couldn't possibly work, not with all the money EMI had to throw around. In the end, I acquiesced. I called my mum to tell her about the trip and to ask her if she would be able to fly out to Paris with Kennedy that weekend. I'd been told that everything would be taken care of by EMI; I'd receive confirmation of all the details later in the week.

In the end, it was all absolutely worth it. My mum and Kennedy flew out from England that weekend. On the flight

Kennedy was given a birthday cake courtesy of Air France. At the airport they were met by a liveried chauffeur, much to my mum's delight, who took them to their hotel on the Champs-Élysées. This was a second-best—though not really, seeing as it probably cost at least four times as much as it would have cost to stay in Disneyland. I'd kicked up a fuss, insistent that we wouldn't stay anywhere else, couldn't they throw some money and wangle a room. As it was, we had two suites, the largest of which I gave to my mum. The three floors, all gilt-work and marble, were connected by a spiral staircase, a drawing-room on the top floor, a lounge, bedroom and study on the floor below and another bedroom on the floor below that. There were balconies from which to look out over the Arc de Triomphe and down the Champs-Élysées. Though my suite only had two floors, it was just as luxurious. When she arrived, my mum ordered a gin-and-tonic and almost died when she got the bill equivalent to about £12. This was to be put to the EMI account, however, as was everything else, including the room service brought up to the dining-room in her suite.

Having worked the Saturday, I'd flown out on the Sunday, and was similarly chauffeured to the hotel, everything having gone without a hitch, the only inconvenience being that I had lost my toiletries on a train thanks to Paul Guerin, with whom I'd been travelling the previous day. When I'd travelled with him in the past he'd admired the black mini flight case I used to carry my toiletries in. He'd mentioned it to his girlfriend and she'd bought him one as a present, only the one she'd bought him was bright green and he wanted a black one like mine. Paul had asked if we could swap cases, just for the journey. I agreed. It was only when I gave him his case after we'd got off the train that he realised he'd left mine on it.

When I arrived at the hotel, however, I found a bag of toiletries waiting for me. Perfume, moisturisers, cleanser—hundreds of pounds worth of cosmetics—everything was there. Also waiting for me was a massive bunch of balloons in the lobby for me to take up to the room, the passes for Disneyland (not week- but year-long) attached, along with another (extravagant and quite beautiful) cake. We drove out to Disneyland, the journey taking over an hour. We decided it would be quicker for us to get the Metro so we gave the driver the week off, which was alright with him. We had a meal with a bunch of Disney characters in one of the restaurants. Mum only went the once to Disneyland, preferring to spend the day walking round Paris, enjoying the cafés and restaurants. The hotel staff thought she had to be a celebrity. Somehow it got around that she was Meat Loaf's mother. The whole week we were treated like royalty, eating off silver service, the staff unable to go to too much trouble. It was a fairytale of a birthday.

*

There were weddings as well as birthdays. I married my first husband Michael in Hesketh Bank, at All Saints Church, on 3 July 1983. It was strange to think, in the run-up to the wedding, of being married there, in the village I had grown up in that now seemed so small after going down to London and crossing continents on tour with all those bands. It was a whirl of preparation. I was touring with Motörhead at the time and finished the week before the wedding. I tried my dress on six days before the wedding. With the physical stress of touring I'd dropped from a size ten to a size eight. I should have informed the dressmaker, who went ballistic when I saw her as she would have just a week in which to take the dress apart and have it remade.

Another concern was who would be showing up on the day. We had invited Black Sabbath, Michael being the bassist Geezer Butler's nephew, and they had confirmed their attendance. My initial encounters with the band hadn't gone too smoothly. I started working with them on their 'Heaven and Hell' tour, the first UK gig of which was played at Portsmouth Guildhall. I was with Jane before the show, counting the merchandise in. As we were doing so, two guys walked into the building carrying bags and made for the auditorium. They tried the doors and found them locked. 'Can I help you?' I said, going over. They started laughing. I asked to see their backstage passes, which only made them laugh the more. I had no idea they were Geezer Butler and Tony Iommi.

Later that evening the tour manager came striding over to the merchandise stall and told us to stop selling the programmes. We asked him why. Because, he said, one of the band members had taken exception to all the other members having *two* pages of the programme devoted to them while he only had *one*. We took the programmes off the stall and didn't sell any the next few nights either. What should have been our day-off we spent sticking an additional page on the slighted band member into every single programme. In the end, however, I got out of this horrendous task by going off to Cornwall with Geezer Butler's nephew instead.

I'd spent quite a lot of time with Black Sabbath over the years, once at Tittenhurst Park when they were recording there. I'd got to see the famous White Room and marvelled at John Lennon and Yoko Ono's having slapped a load of white paint over such a lovely room. Brian May showed up during rehearsals. I hadn't been without apprehension at the thought of the band descending on my home village, thinking how it would make the wedding a different sort of occasion. Part of me liked the thought of a rock 'n' roll spectacle but part of me wanted it to be just family and friends, a simple beautiful day, without newspapermen and members of the public poking their noses in. Wanting it both ways, I was hoping we could keep quiet that they would be there. This hope was soon scotched, however, when we started getting calls from the papers asking for information about the wedding: Were Black Sabbath going to be there? Who else would be there? (And crucially:) What was the date? Other guests were being pestered too. Envisioning a free-for-all outside the church, I was having second thoughts about the band's attendance. They were thinking the same. In the end, only Geezer Butler and his wife Gloria were with us on the day.

I had been to their wedding in St Louis. It was the only wedding I've ever been to wearing jeans and a sweatshirt, Michael only slightly more casual in his jeans and a plain black T-shirt. We were all in excellent, if slightly hysterical, spirits. We were laughing so much that it took a tremendous effort of will for Geezer and Gloria to get through the vows. From the registry office we went to a restaurant for a fabulous dinner. It was there that I heard the story of how they met.

They had met in St Louis. Black Sabbath were flying in for a gig. This piece of information had been acquired by Gloria, who had never met Geezer but was eager to contrive an encounter and initiate romance. To this end, she had roped in one of her friends and hired a Porsche which her friend would drive to the airport to meet her as she strutted out of arrivals, dressed to the nines, just as Geezer was doing the same. They would meet and their life together would begin.

Unfortunately, despite the meticulousness of Gloria's planning, things didn't quite work out. After a fumbled exchange,

Geezer had got into his car and was whisked away out of the airport. Gloria jumped in the Porsche and told her friend to give chase. Ripping out of the car park, they kept Geezer's limousine in sight and eventually managed to push through the congested roads and get behind it. It was when the limousine stopped that Gloria, determined not to miss another opportunity, had the idea of ramming the Porsche into it. Her friend asked if she was sure. 'Do it,' said Gloria, and she dutifully rammed the limousine. They climbed out of their vehicles and gathered by the roadside, Gloria apologising profusely on behalf of her dangerously careless friend, making sure that no one was hurt, making a big fuss over Geezer, and so their life together, after the small hiccup of not-quite-beginning, began.

It was perhaps just as well that it was only Geezer and Gloria at the wedding. While relationships within the band were generally pretty good, those between their spouses weren't always so. There was a lot of rivalry, jealousy and cattiness. They would always be telling each other what they were wearing—Dior, Chanel—each trying to outdo the others. I noticed, over time, how the dynamics within the band changed. Tensions arose and tempers flared more quickly. When it was just the band, they were a tight unit. It was when they were joined by their spouses that things turned sour. Wanting the best for their husbands, and not having anything else to do, they'd start making demands on their behalf. 'Why aren't his shirts ironed?' 'Why isn't his costume ready?' 'How come his food isn't here yet?' Things that wouldn't have been an issue suddenly became an issue because their wives were devoted to making them one.

I'll always remember the time Gloria decided to buy Geezer a Mercedes for his birthday. She mentioned this to Ronnie James Dio's wife, who, with Ronnie's birthday coming up, thought he might like one too, though she'd of course have to do one better, and so got the next model up—a convertible. When Gloria found out, she decided Geezer had better have the convertible too, only he'd have it with custom white-leather upholstery. Well then Ronnie had better have the white-leather upholstery too, and what about an upgrade to the engine? So it went on… Geezer's car was delivered, fresh from the showroom, the paintwork gleaming, a bow tied over the bonnet. For all the trouble Gloria had gone to, he didn't seem all that pleased. Ronnie expressed similarly when he got his. Who, after all, was getting the bill?

It was another American wedding, this one in Los Angeles, that gave me my Pretty Woman moment. It was going to be a grand wedding. I was in Hesketh Bank, just back from a tour, and would be flying out from Heathrow on the Monday. It was quarter-to-five on Saturday evening and I needed an outfit. There was a clothes shop (now a chocolate shop) in Tarleton, the village next to Hesketh Bank, and I dashed down there to see if I could find something, having no chance the following day when the shops would be shut. I arrived at ten-to-five, still wearing my T-shirt, jeans and trainers, not having had time to change. I went in and said that I was looking for something for a wedding. The proprietress told me they were closed. I said it was ten-to-five. She told me that's when the shop closes. I said the sign on the door says five. She said she was closing early. I took the hint and shook the dust from my trainers on my way out.

Thankfully I had a friend who owned a clothes shop not too far away, so I went over there and picked out a designer suit costing £500. (This was in 1990.) Admiring the cut of the suit, I was delighted not to have given the snobbish proprietress my custom and knew just what I would do when I got back from LA. Exhausted after the flight but thrilling at the prospect of comeuppance, I walked into the little clothes shop in my exquisite suit, casting my eyes over the garments as one who has no need to look at the price tags. Noticing the proprietress eyeing me as she hung a lacy dress, I made my way over. 'You refused to serve me,' I said. Allowing her to appreciate what I had bought instead, I said those words that every woman dreams of saying once in her life:

'*Big* mistake. Big. Huge!'

And with that, I turned on my heel and walked out of the shop, never to set foot in it again.

One of my best shopping experiences was in Paris when I went on a bit of a spree after my luggage failed to arrive with me. I'd just flown in from LA, where I had had a great time, back to rainy London, taking a Hertz hire car from Heathrow back up north for my Mum's birthday. I was at the Hertz centre when I got a call from the management of Credit to the Nation telling me the group had been asked to perform at a music awards ceremony in Paris (the first I'd heard), could I fly out there? I told them I'd just got back from Catalina and that I was going home for my mum's birthday. They asked me what day my mum's birthday was and told me I'd be back in time. I said they might have mentioned it sooner. Yes, well...

Would I still go? I told them I didn't have any luggage, my bag hadn't got on the plane. Fine, they said, we'll give you money to buy clothes. And make-up, I said, I don't have my make-up. Don't worry, they said, have some more money to buy make-up. I wasn't trying to take advantage of the management's generosity, I was making excuses like I had been over Kennedy's birthday, only for the obstacles I threw up to be dissolved by the company's ultra-high liquidity. In the end, out of excuses other than not wanting to go, I gave in. I left the Hertz centre and got on a plane to Paris, a shopping spree on the Champs-Élysées in prospect. I couldn't deny there were perks to the job. The awards show was, as you'd expect, a great spectacle, hosted by a troop of supermodels, attended by their extensive entourages. Linda Evangelista was there, as was Kyle MacLachlan. I remember bumping into Louise Redknapp, who was appearing with Eternal. It was a vast assembly of celebrity royalty. There were so many acts, each dressing room shared with about five other bands.

*

It was the day before the first anniversary of mine and my second husband's wedding. I was in Canada, on tour with Concrete Blonde. Paul, having just finished a tour with Bryan Adams, flew out to meet me, bringing a huge bunch of white roses and a magnum of champagne with him. (By this time, after all the complementary bottles left in hotel rooms, champagne was my drink of choice.) Still having a lot of work to do, I said I would go up to my room to get it done, and, leaving him to have a drink in the bar, said I would see him later.

A while later, I was in my room speaking on the phone when Johnette knocked on the door and came in. When I got off the phone she started telling me she had seen a really cute guy in the bar and that she'd gone over to chat him up. He didn't seem all that interested. She asked if she could buy him a drink. He said he was good. She carried on talking, hoping he'd show some interest. He didn't. She went on for a while longer before the penny dropped. Shit, I thought; she's talking about Paul. Johnette was saying this 'really cute guy' was looking at her as though he were thinking 'Who *is* this woman?' Perhaps he's not into girls, she said. Perhaps not, I said, knowing otherwise. But, Johnette said, she had a pretty good sense and she sensed that he *was* into girls. Just not her, it seemed. What did I make of that? Before I could reply there was a knock on the door and Paul walked in.

'Paul,' I said. 'This is Johnette.'

*

I've always enjoyed seeing in the New Year. The year that Geezer Butler came to stay with me and my husband in Hesketh Bank, though, I was quite nervous. Not because I had any problem with him, but because I was wondering what he would make of my house, my friends, the village. We went for a drink at the Becconsall Hotel (since shut-down and later demolished) which was just down the road from us. We drank a lot of whisky and I felt terrible the next day, though I blamed it on something I'd eaten. We had a lovely grand piano in the house and my standout memory of Geezer's stay was his playing it almost all the time we were in the house.

A rather more unusual New Year's Eve party was at the comedian Jasper Carrott's. Bev Bevan, ELO's drummer who had been touring with Black Sabbath, was co-hosting. Bev and Jasper, at the front door to greet everyone as they arrived, had evidently gone to a lot of trouble. There would be about a hundred of us in all. I had thought it would be drinks and nibbles. As I stepped through the hallway, though, I could see that it was to be a sit-down dinner—for one hundred people. There were tables everywhere, in the hallway, the lounge, the dining room, laid with silver cutlery and crystal glassware. After the excellent meal, glasses were charged and we sang 'Auld Lang Syne' to the accompaniment of bagpipes played by Roy Wood from Wizzard. It was a decidedly odd but quite incredible party, one of the best I've ever been to.

The *best* New Year's Eve party I ever went to, though, was in Southern Ireland when I was with the Waterboys. We were staying at a hotel out in the sticks. The band played an incredible gig that night, a show of such intense celebration it couldn't have happened anywhere else. We got back to the hotel and found a party in full swing—booze flowing, music blaring, the receptionists dancing on the reception desks. Everyone joined the party, guests and staff together. There was a constant circulation of people and a constant circulation of bottles amongst them. If you want a drink, we were told, just go behind the bar, help yourself, here's how you work the till. No one went to bed, the doors stayed open all night. A breakfast was served late the next morning, a help-yourself full Irish. With plenty of booze to soak up, we tucked in, the hotel staff, including the chefs, joining us, just as hungover as we were.

There was no one else staying at the hotel and we were having such a good time we decided we'd stay another night, partying all the way through New Year's Day too. Again, we were told to help ourselves, drinks behind the bar, food in the kitchens, plates of sandwiches brought out in the afternoon, the breakfast left out all day. We collapsed into our beds on 2nd January. That evening, we said goodbye to the staff and thanked them for the best New Year's of our lives. If that beginning was anything to go by, it looked like it was going to be a very good year.

6

America

It was a Friday evening I got a call from Doug Smith telling me that Paul Bolton from the agency was going to call me, about something, Paul would tell me what, in about two minutes. Deflecting my requests for elaboration, he said goodbye and hung up.

A couple of minutes later the phone rang again. Paul Bolton was on the line. He told me he'd recently spoken with an American colleague, Frank Volpe, who was looking for a female tour manager for Concrete Blonde. I asked why female. Paul told me that the band had gone through a number of tour managers—all of them male— and that Johnette Napolitano, the lead singer, had asked Frank to see if he could find a female tour manager. At the time there weren't many of these around—six, to be precise. Four of these women were tour managers in virtue of their husbands being so; the other two were tied to particular bands. Paul and Doug, when asked if they knew of anyone, had both put my name forward. Paul said that Frank would call me in five minutes to tell me more.

Five minutes later Frank Volpe called. He repeated what Paul had told me about Concrete Blonde wanting to try a female tour manager. 'I understand you've worked with Motörhead,' he said. Ten years, I told him. 'That's what Doug told me,' he said. 'I figured if you've spent ten years with Motörhead, this'll be a walk in the park.'

And that was it: my interview. I'd got the job. I was going to America.

*

Before I flew out I took a two-day crash course in tour-management. The first day I spent with Doug Smith going through contracts, the second day shadowing Chris Healy. Chris was an inspiration. A lovely man, never flustered, great company. At the end of the course, however, I felt I knew less than I knew before. I wasn't having second thoughts—no *way* was I going to turn this opportunity down—but I was definitely apprehensive. The single piece of advice Doug and Chris had both left me with was: if you have a problem, call one of us. My visa was obtained, my flight booked and my contract came through. I didn't know whether I was being paid the same wages as would have been paid to a man. I didn't ask because I didn't care. I would be getting $3,000 per week plus $200 for expenses plus a per diem. I'd never earned this much money before.

Shortly before I was due to leave I got a call from Frank asking me what piece I'd like to carry over there.

'Piece?' I said.

'Yeah, piece,' he said. 'Gun.'

'Gun?!' I said, 'I don't need a gun.'

'You sure?'

'I'm sure,' I said.

I'd been reminded that America wasn't England, that it was a larger, wilder place. Still, I wasn't going to carry a gun. Never having fired a gun in my life, I reckoned that should I ever find myself in a situation in which I might conceivably need one, chances are the person I'd be needing it against would be carrying one too— and would be much more adept than me. Whatever they asked me for, I'd give them. I did, however, think it would probably be worth taking some lessons in self-defence, so I sought out an instructor in Penwortham, a suburb outside Preston. I told him I was going to America and wanted to learn how to defend myself should the need arise. He asked me when I was going. Tuesday, I said. (This was the Friday before.) He laughed. He wasn't offended that I'd presumed I could be taught the art he must have spent years mastering in a matter of days, though I supposed he had every right to be. It wasn't quite a crash course he gave me, but he did give me some excellent tips.

First, he showed me how to break various bones in an assailant's body (nose, kneecaps, feet). Second, he told me that ninety percent of crimes committed in hotels are committed by hotel staff, the reason being that they have access to the guest book and are thus able to see who's staying there and whose room might be worth visiting. Silly aliases were just as bad as real names. Donald Duck in room 285 would likely be worth a try. He recommended that I take a man's T-shirt with me, size extra-large, some boxer shorts and socks, and scatter these around the hotel room when I went in. If anyone was to enter the room, seeing these items of clothing lying about, they would assume I'd sneaked someone in with me. I followed this piece of advice on numerous occasions. If I was staying a couple of days in a hotel, I'd hang the clothes on the radiator to make it look as though my chunky companion was still there with me.

So, with my short courses in tour-management and self-defence, I spent the weekend at home and flew out to America the following Tuesday. Flying over the Atlantic, sipping a gin-and-tonic, Los Angeles-bound, I felt I'd made it. We touched down in LAX and I went through customs, stepping through to arrivals and scanning the placards for my name. Not seeing it, I stood to one side to wait for whoever was collecting me to show up. The placards dropped as arrivals met collectors, the room emptying.

I'd been waiting about half-an-hour when I looked over at a young woman still waiting for her arrival. I peered over at her placard but couldn't make out the name on it. Noticing me looking at her, she stared back at me. From her expression, it seemed she wasn't expecting me. Eventually, we were the only ones left. I went over to her. Seeing my name on her card, I said that's me, relieved and rather embarrassed. She looked up and down, a doubtful expression on her face. 'You are?' she said. 'Yes,' I said, 'I'm Kim.' She knew Kim was a woman but she had been expecting someone big and butch and thought I couldn't possibly have been her. We drove to Frank's office. Bob Engel, who ran the agency Concrete Blonde worked for, was there too. After we'd introduced ourselves and chit-chatted a while, we got down to business. Frank said I would need to create an itinerary for the tour. This was something I hadn't done before and which Paul and Doug hadn't talked me through. Determined, however, to make a good first impression, I got down to it. Within a week I'd got an itinerary together. Then we went on the road.

*

When I'd worked in the States before, as a merchandiser, I hadn't enjoyed it all that much. This was partly down to my age. Being nineteen or twenty, I was too young to go the bars and clubs that everybody else was going to and so I ended up spending many long evenings on my own in my hotel room. Partly it was down to our playing a lot of stadium gigs. We'd be travelling during the day and when we got to the venue the bus would often drive straight into these artificially-lit concrete caverns. (When you see rock stars wearing sunglasses, often they're not just shielding their eyes from unwanted attention, they're shielding it from the glaring daylight they can go for days without seeing.) This meant there was little opportunity for sightseeing. One time I remember we were going to San Francisco. I was so excited. I went up the bus to the driver's cabin and asked him how long till we would be there. He looked at me askance and said we'd been there three days ago. I was gutted. Because we often drove overnight, on those occasions when there was something I wanted to see and I knew where I was, it wasn't possible to see anything in the dark. 'There's the Hoover Dam,' the driver would say, 'though you can't actually see it...' 'We're on Highway 66, shame you can't see it...' 'Niagara Falls is just over there, only you won't be able to see it...'

I was determined, therefore, that in my new role I'd see everything I'd missed. Whenever we arrived in a new place, I'd take twenty minutes out of my packed schedule to go sightseeing. Twenty minutes wasn't much but it was all I could afford. I'd get in a taxi and say to the driver, 'Right. I've got twenty minutes before I need to be back here. Show me all the sights you can.' And off we'd go, returning to the venue twenty minutes later, and I'd have seen at least some of the local attractions. Sometimes surprisingly many. I remember my taxi-tour of San Francisco. 'There's the Bridge... there's Alcatraz... there's Pier 39... there's a street car...'

Later, when I'd given up tour-managing, I used to take my daughter on these taxi-tours. Not having the money I'd had when I was touring, I couldn't afford long spells at the luxurious hotels I'd once stayed at, meals at the five-star restaurants I'd once eaten in, but, not being able to bear the thought of taking Kennedy somewhere and having memories of having been somewhere much better before, we used to take mini breaks together, stopping just one night in a city and living it up. Often with just an afternoon, we'd have had no chance of doing all our sightseeing on foot.

The time I did spend in hotels when I was tour-managing was even more comfortable than when I'd been a merchandiser. Almost invariably I would be given the best suites. I had a ritual I performed whenever I entered a hotel room. First, I would set down my suitcase and briefcase by the door, holding it open before walking inside, looking over the room, behind the curtains, inside wardrobes, under the bed. I would poke my head inside the bathroom, then I would close the door. All the leaflets left out—room service information, restaurant cards, tourist brochures—I'd gather up and stick in a drawer so when it was time to leave I'd know that all the papers left out on top were mine so there was no chance I'd end up leaving some crucial document behind. I never unpacked my suitcase, only removing a toiletries bag which I'd stick straight in the bathroom.

As it turned out, the self-defence instructor from Penwortham had been right to caution me about staying in hotels. Sometimes, when we had an overnight drive, we would book day rooms so that everyone could get off the bus, relax, shower, have a sleep, have something to eat. One time we had a couple of day rooms booked and arrived at the hotel about 11 am. The rooms were on the executive floor which could only be accessed with a key. In such cases we'd ask for several keys to share between us, four or five keys to a room. Always being the first to go up, I went to check the rooms over. In one of them I'd set down my bag and the door had closed behind me. The next moment there was a knock on the door. Thinking it was one of the band, I went to open it and found a big man stood outside. When I say big, I mean *big*. Seven-foot tall, bear-like. He asked me where Kim was, Kim Stewart, said he needed to speak to him. On this occasion I thanked goodness that once again my name had been mistaken for a man's. I said I thought Kim hadn't come up yet, he was probably downstairs, then I slammed the door in his face and called down to reception and asked for security. They searched the building top to bottom. No sign of him. The hotel staff were so perturbed they decided to call the police. What was especially worrying was that he'd known my name (he'd asked for Kim Stewart, not just Kim). Not only must he have known that the band were staying at the hotel, he knew that I was responsible for them. I was assigned a police escort for the duration of my stay.

Later in the day, we were outside the hotel and a guy came up to me asking if I was with Concrete Blonde. I said yes. He said that he was a clairvoyant and that he had a reading for Johnette Napolitano which he thought she'd be interested to hear. Could I speak to Johnette's manager and pass on the message for him. Aware that I was Johnette's manager and that the clairvoyant hadn't managed to divine the fact, one of the police escorts looked him in the eye and said in the most wonderful southern drawl, 'Hey boy, I think yer in the wrong line of business.'

There was another occasion when the assumption that 'Kim' was a man proved advantageous. Arriving early at a venue one afternoon, I took a seat on some flight cases near the bar area and waited for the others to arrive. The promoter went up to the girl behind the bar and asked if they had a bottle of an expensive tequila Johnette had requested. Looking over the bottles, the girl said they had other tequilas but the only bottle of that brand they had was empty. The promoter told her to fill it with a bottle of another tequila, which the girl did, handing over the bottle. 'They're not going to notice,' he said.

Later in the day I walked into his office. 'Can I help you?' he said. 'Yes,' I said, 'I think we need to change this,' and handed him the tequila bottle. His face, now red, dropped. 'Of course,' he said, taking the bottle. Perhaps we wouldn't have noticed the switch. We'd have been highly unlikely not to have noticed the broken seal, however. As it was, I'd seen everything. He'd had no idea who I was. This wasn't the only time I saw or heard things I wasn't meant to see or hear—all thanks to my name.

That inept clairvoyant aside, Johnette had a lot of time for the supernatural. She was good friends with the Gothic novelist Anne

Rice, with whom I once had a very pleasant conversation over the phone having invited her to a Concrete Blonde gig. Johnette had told me of the time she stayed at the Driskill Hotel, notorious for being the most haunted hotel in Texas, in the most haunted of the rooms, number 525. It's said that in the bathroom, on the same night twenty years apart, two brides committed suicide. Johnette woke in the night to find a Texan gentleman sat at the end of her bed. She was convinced he was the ghost of Colonel Jesse Driskill, the Tennessean entrepreneur who'd built the hotel and lost it in a game of poker. The experience inspired her to write the song 'Ghost of a Texas Ladies Man'. Johnette wasn't the only singer to have come across a spirit at the Driskill. Annie Lennox, when she was staying there, had put out two dresses on her bed, undecided between which to wear, before taking a shower. When she returned to the bedroom, she found that one of the dresses had been put away, a Driskill ghost apparently having made the decision for her.

We were booked to stay at the hotel while we were in Texas. Johnette had insisted that she stay in the same room (number 525) and had been going on about the Driskill ghosts for days, anticipating another encounter. I'd been pooh-poohing her, but that night, after the gig, walking through the low-lit hotel with its dark heavy furnishings, I began to feel distinctly ill at ease, so much so that I decided I wasn't going to bed. Chris Bailey, the support act, didn't want to go to bed either, so we kept each other company in the bar. This was the first tour I'd done with Chris. He reminded me of the end of the first night when I'd been in the office, finishing the accounts and he'd caught me smiling to myself. He'd asked me what I was smiling about. Nothing, I'd said, my smile widening. Go on, he'd said. I'd said I would tell him at the end of the tour, which was what I said again that night.

It was 4 am and me and Chris were the last ones in the bar. The barman was wanting to close for the night. With no alternative, we reluctantly went up to our rooms. I unlocked my door and switched on the light. I always slept with the light on and this night of nights I wasn't going to break the habit. Cautiously, I entered the room, looking about me, straining to catch any untoward stirrings. I sat down on the bed and, without undressing, without even taking off my shoes, I lay down on it, my eyes wide open. My cases were by the door, I hadn't even taken out my toiletries bag, so that should any apparition appear I could grab my things and be out of the room in an instant.

A knock on the door.

My heart banged in my chest.

I was deliberating whether to answer it when I heard Johnette say my name. I went to the door and opened it. Johnette looked as if she had seen the Colonel again. She hadn't, she said, and didn't want to. Could she please stay in my room? Alright, I said, my heart returning to something like a normal rhythm, thinking I might have a chance of getting some sleep having Johnette with me—which was a mistake. She kept on with her ghost stories, ignoring my telling her to leave it alone. She then produced a pack of Tarot cards and proceeded to turn them out on the bedspread. I rolled over and did my best to ignore her. As the sun came up, my fear ebbed. We grabbed a quick breakfast and checked out early.

I had another haunting experience with Johnette on Halloween. Next door to the venue the band were playing was a disused building which a bunch of students had converted into a haunted house. This is quite common in the States. They really go for it—designing costumes, acting the parts. They'd done a very good job with this haunted house. It was worthy of Alton Towers. In fact, they'd done rather *too* good a job. It was while Johnette was signing autographs outside the venue after the show (something she always did) that a couple of the students asked her if she'd like to pay a visit. She would, she said, and asked me if she could. The students said that if she were to wait an hour or so she could have a look round when they had closed to visitors. That sounded fine. What didn't sound so fine was Johnette's asking me to go with her. Despite my apprehension, I said I would, making sure to fetch the massive Maglite torch I carried round with me at venues, using it to find my way around murky backstage areas and to send signals across the auditorium, as well as to shine into the eyes of any threatening person I might stumble across. The last autograph signed, we made our way over to the haunted house. It really did look haunted. As we cautiously proceeded through the house, looking over our shoulders as we went, I sensed someone jump out from a dark corner as they made to grab me. 'Please don't do that,' I said, petrified. Then, thinking quickly, indicating Johnette, I said, 'I'm her minder and I might hit you if you do that again.' I asked him to pass the message along to his ghoulish mates ahead of us.

One of my most unnerving experiences was at the Hollywood Roosevelt Hotel, another famously haunted hotel. We were staying in the cabana rooms looking onto the Tropicana bar and pool. Marilyn Monroe used to stay in one of these and see JFK when he was in town, the car access conducing to discreet assignations. In a mirror that was hung in the foyer people have claimed to have seen Marilyn looking out at them. Johnette had been harping on ghosts again and playing with a small child's Ouija board earlier in the day, asking the board where Harry, the drummer, who was always munching on something, could find something to eat. The board responded: the third drawer on the bedside table. Harry opened the drawer and found the chocolate bar Johnette had hidden there beforehand and duly freaked out. For all the joking around, however, I felt uneasy. That it was Halloween contributed to my disquiet. I woke in the middle of the night to a furious crackling sound. A light was flickering on the ceiling. I bolted upright. The TV was switched on. I jumped out of bed, turned it off and jumped back into bed, pulling the covers up to my chin.

(Why *do* you feel so suddenly safe in bed?)

With the morning came not only the spirit-defying light but the Roosevelt's prodigious breakfast. I was far from alone in considering it the best of any hotel breakfast in the world. Everything you might have wanted was on offer. Whatever sort of omelette you wanted, you'd get at the omelette bar. Ditto for waffles at the waffle bar and for pancakes at the pancake bar. Fruit, muffins, toast, pastries, savouries—you fancied it, it was there. Bands always used to look forward to staying at the Hollywood Roosevelt for the breakfast. If it was a late night, you'd stay up so you wouldn't miss it.

The last night of the Concrete Blonde tour came along. Chris got up with his acoustic guitar to play his set. One of his songs had a trumpet solo on the album version. Not having a trumpet player with him on tour, when he came to this part, he used to say, 'Trumpet solo,' and carry on playing, letting the audience play the solo in their heads. On this occasion, however, when he said, 'Trumpet solo,' he was surprised to introduce not a solo trumpet but a trio of trumpets, courtesy of Johnette who had gone and bought sombreros and a set of plastic toy trumpets for the purpose. They didn't have a great sound—something like a kazoo—but it was a novelty, the three of us gathered round the microphone, tooting away.

At the end of shows pizzas were often ordered. Johnette loved pizza but, because she was on a strict diet while she was on tour, had to wait until the end of a tour before she could have any. We'd ordered a special pizza for her and I, who because of my accent and my always telling everyone what to do she used to call 'the Queen', was to make a special presentation of it. Unfortunately, the pizza didn't turn up. Having gone to such trouble, we didn't want to miss the opportunity. While someone was trying to call the pizzeria and find out what had happened, someone else had noticed something in one of the bins—a pizza box containing a cold half-eaten pizza left by one of the security guards. Waste not, want not, he'd pulled it out and brought it through. While doubtful of its edibility, we decided that the symbolism was enough, and so, wheeled in on a trolley dressed in a flowing ballgown, waving a royal hand, with a magnanimous flourish I presented Johnette with the half-eaten pizza. None of us thought she would eat it. She did.

What I'd been smiling to myself about when Chris Bailey came into the office after that first successful show and which I'd promised to tell him at the end of the tour, was that I had never worked as a tour manager in the States before. After that last gig, he asked me once more what my secret was. I told him. I hadn't told anyone else, having enough doubts of my own and not wanting to have other people's piled on top. At first he didn't believe me. Which is just what I'd have hoped. America, as I'd thought and as it proved to be, was something else. Yet I'd done it.

*

Having spent a lot of time in America before I went over there as a tour manager, I didn't have to make any great adjustments. That being said, there were still things that surprised me, things I could never get used to. One of these was holidays. So many of them. Christmas I used to find very strange. You could go out and do things on Christmas Day—go to the cinema, see a show. While the shops would usually be closed, it was only for the day. On Thanksgiving, however, *everything* was closed. I'd gone out for some wine and found the streets deserted, shop windows dark.

Another thing was the scale of the place, the huge distances you'd travel as a matter of course, planes used like buses. Tachographs had been introduced in Europe to monitor the time drivers spent at the wheels of their vehicles. In America, they hadn't, and the drivers just used to drive and drive. The longest journey lasted three days. At the end of it we arrived in a little town, probably the smallest I've ever visited. The local economy can't have been large, supported by just three establishments, the needs of the inhabitants apparently few—a twelve-room motel, a casino and a sex shop. The only place to get a bite to eat was the casino.

I used to enjoy overnight drives. One of my favourite things was staying up with a driver called Tom, a good man and a good friend. It would have been another manic day and by 3 or 4 am, when everyone else had fallen into bed, there would be a most wonderful state of calm. Usually I didn't eat during the day—I didn't have time—so we'd pull up at a truck stop and Tom and I would go down to get something to eat. My usual meal (which the Americans didn't seem to think much of) was egg and chips. We'd take our trays back onto the bus and enjoy a peaceful supper.

Such a simple thing—eating cheap trucker's fare in the company of a friend—was a treat amidst the constant luxury. It's surprising how dissatisfying the best of everything can become. I was used to handling large sums of money but in America they were even larger. I was always paid in cash and—partly because my expenses and per diems were so generous, partly because I simply didn't have time—I always had a lot on me. Sometimes I'd stuff it into bags which I would tape round my stomach and conceal under a T-shirt, sometimes I'd strap on multiple money belts. The most money I ever had at one time was in Las Vegas. The floor of my hotel room was covered in rolls of bills. It took five hours to count it all up. There was $750,000. I remember thinking wryly to myself that, in that swanky hotel, I was probably the poorest person on my floor.

There were times, however, when the best simply wasn't available. The worst motel I ever stayed in was in Austin, Texas, when I was there for SXSW, the annual festival to which everyone in the music industry flocks. My room was horrid. Truly horrid. I could smell the damp as soon as I opened the door. Stale cigarette smoke too. I stepped inside and felt a horrible sucking sensation as my shoes stuck to the carpet. Immediately I felt incredibly dirty. There was no chance I was taking anything out of my cases. I spread a sheet over the bed so I could lie down without touching the bedspread. I smoked at the time and I decided to have a cigarette, only I couldn't find my lighter. I looked around to see if there were any matches lying around and opened a drawer to find it *full* of cigarette ends. No matches. I went to the bathroom to wash my hands. All the surfaces were sticky. Somehow I managed to get some sleep.

In the morning I got a call from Doug Smith. 'We're leaving,' he said. I asked him where we were going, thinking there couldn't possibly be rooms available anywhere else, the city being overrun for the festival. He said he'd found some rooms at the Sheraton Hotel. Expensive, he said, but there we were, there was no way he was staying on at the motel. I asked him what had made the motel all of a sudden so inhospitable. He told me he'd been doing some paperwork and dropped his pen. Bending down to retrieve it, he had seen something poking out from under the bed. He had looked closer and found a human finger. It was like something from *No Country for Old Men*. Having put down the phone, I was out of my room in a moment, delighted to be leaving. I was so glad that it was Doug who had found the finger in his room—not just because it meant that it wasn't me who found it, but because if it had been anyone else and they'd insisted on moving elsewhere, he would almost certainly have told them it wasn't such a big deal and not to be so dramatic, that it wasn't worth blowing the budget we had for hotels—as he did.

Speaking of trouble with hotels, I remember going to a great deal of trouble altering guitarist Marc Morland's hotel bookings. I'd got to know him while he was working with Pretty and Twisted. He and Johnette Napolitano, with whom he'd formed the band in the mid '90s, were very close. The one thing he couldn't abide was lifts. He simply couldn't use them. All the hotel rooms that had been booked on any other floor than the ground floor had to be changed for ground-floor rooms. It was either that or find him another hotel.

The worst flight I've ever been on was from Austin to New York. It was packed, almost all the passengers airline staff. It was pouring with rain when we took off and pouring with rain when we came in to JFK airport. Out of the window I saw a sign for Toys "R" Us on the left. We hit the runway and then we were back in the air.

Vertical. There was a collective gasp and burst of profanity as we turned to each other, wondering what the hell had just happened. All eyes were wide, faces white. The plane became horizontal again and we circled back for another descent and touched down, this time staying on the runway and taxiing to the gate. The moment the cabin doors were opened everyone rushed off the plane without collecting their bags, hurrying through the terminal to get outside for a cigarette, smokers and non-smokers alike, oblivious to the still-pouring rain. Cigarettes were shared and lit and you could see composure gradually regained. I followed the staring eyes of some fellow passengers and saw the pilot stumbling away from the plane, his shirt unbuttoned to his stomach, his tie yanked down. I don't know what had precipitated the evasive action but the state he was in told all too plainly how close a shave it must have been.

I spent a lot of time in New York. With its immensity, populousness and febrile energy, it felt the centre of the world. The downside to this is the time it takes to get anywhere. For the most part, I was able to cope. Congestion, traffic lights, overflowing sidewalks, I could handle. It was lifts that got to me. Meeting someone in the lobby of your hotel in five minutes—forget it. You could spend ten or fifteen minutes waiting to squeeze into a crammed lift and then it would take another small eternity to get you all the way down the God-only-knows-how-many floors. As in other major cities, it was amazing who'd turn up at shows. Nick Cave used to come to a lot of Concrete Blonde gigs. One evening I remember going to the promoter's office and seeing a guy leaning against the wall outside, one foot resting on it, headphones on, his head bobbing to whatever was piping through them. I had no idea who he was. If I'd known it was Lenny Kravitz (as the promoter told me afterwards), I would have said hello.

One of the things we used to do when bands arrived for the first time in New York was take them up the Twin Towers. We'd do this early in the morning and look out at the sleepless city. Then 9/11 happened. I was in New York shortly afterwards, when the President was there and the city was shut-down. I thought of the times I'd stayed in the hotel in the Towers complex, looking where the Towers had stood and seeing what lay behind them. In cafes and restaurants nearby, there were half-eaten meals left on empty tables, handbags abandoned by empty chairs. I remember thinking that the passengers on those planes couldn't have known what was about to happen. The reason I believe this is that I know a team of riggers had been on one of the planes. While I didn't know these guys personally, I've known a lot of riggers in my time. They're a fearless bunch, scaling rigs, dangling like monkeys, many of them without harnesses in the days before health and safety. These guys would have been sat together on the plane. I'm sure that had they known what was going on, they wouldn't have stayed in their seats. It was so terribly surreal, so unbearably sad. Yet you could sense, in spite of the violence and upheaval, a clear determination that life would go on. As it did, and has gone on.

7

Toilet Tales

Open the pages of any rock 'n' roll memoir and you will come across a story involving a hotel room, the police and a dash for the toilet. This book is an exception, but only insofar as it contains *two* such stories. Taken together, they throw into relief the light and the dark of the business of rock 'n' roll. The first story is unmatched—certainly I have never come across anything to match it—for its lunatic convolutions. The second is almost as ridiculous, though not *nearly* as funny.

*

I was in the States with Concrete Blonde and the tour had not been without its strains. One of the chief causes of discontent was James Mankey's NordicTrack elliptical cross trainer, which he had insisted on bringing aboard the tour bus. Jim was obsessed with fitness and was loathe to succumb to the unhealthy habits of life on the road.

The cross trainer, having been delivered to one of the venues, was loaded onto the bus and took up the whole of the aisle, so that if you wanted to get to the lounge at the back you had to climb over it to do so. (Not so bad if you're long-limbed, but quite an inconvenience if you're not—especially if you've had a few.) When Jim did his workouts, the cross trainer had to be dragged down to the front of the bus where he would spend an hour or two pumping and puffing. For all the frustration it caused everyone else, it was probably a good thing for Jim to have an outlet for his own. On the whole, he was quiet and calm, but just occasionally he'd lose it, and when he blew, he blew.

We were in New Orleans and—blessed thing—had a late start. When we stopped off at a hotel, I would stick a note under each person's door detailing the schedule for the duration of our stay. The notes I had stuck under everyone's doors the night before had seen that they were informed that we didn't have to leave the hotel till three, so everyone would be able to enjoy a much-needed lie-in. I had been enjoying mine when I was woken by a fierce knocking on my door. Fearing that in my exhaustion I'd managed to oversleep, I looked at my bedside clock. It was 10am. I went to the door and found Jim outside, fully dressed, ready for the day, his suitcase beside him.

'Where was my wake-up call?' he fired.

'Your what?' I said, squinting at him with sleep-drunk eyes.

'My wake-up call. I didn't have my wake-up call.'

'Jim, it's ten o'clock.'

'I know it's ten o'clock. If I'd had my wake-up call, I'd have been ready on time.'

'On time?'

'Yes. *On time.*' He looked up and down the corridor. 'Where the hell is everybody?'

'I suspect they're in bed.'

'In bed?'

'Where I was.'

'Jesus Christ! What chance has anyone got when the wake-up caller needs a fucking wake-up call?'

'Didn't you see my note?'

'Your note?'

'My note.'

'What note?'

'The schedule I put under your door.'

He said nothing, but from the way he shifted on his feet I gathered that he hadn't.

'It's on the schedule I put under everyone's doors that we aren't leaving the hotel till three this afternoon.'

He didn't look happy about this.

'So we're not leaving till three?'

'No.'

'You're fucking kidding me.'

'No, I'm not. What's the big problem?'

'I've already checked out.'

'Why did you do that?'

'Why do you think I did that?'

'Well, we won't be leaving till three. Everyone will be making the most of their lie-in, as I'd had in mind to do.'

'Well what am I supposed to do now then?'

'You'll just have to wait.'

'Wait? Wait where?'

'Go down to the lobby. Read a book. Have a cappuccino.'

'For five hours?'

Five hours was a long time to wait, and I didn't fancy seeing what state he would be in at the end of it. I said I would call down to reception and see if I could get him his room back. 'Come in if you don't want to stand in the hall,' I said. He said he would stand in the hall.

I called down to reception and asked if Jim could have his room back. The receptionist told me that, as Mr Mankey's room would not yet have been cleaned, that wasn't a problem; he could collect his keys from reception. I thanked the receptionist and relayed the good news to Jim, telling him that he could leave his suitcase with me if he didn't want to take it back down to reception only to bring it up again. 'No thank you,' he snapped. He snatched up his suitcase and bustled down the hallway, muttering as he went.

When we met in the lobby later that afternoon, Jim was his usual cool self. Thereafter he was never in error about the schedule.

Another source of concern, which I had decided it was simply best not to think about, was the fact that one of our backline technicians, who was from England, was working without a visa. He had been working with another band before he joined the Concrete Blonde tour and since there hadn't been time to obtain a new temporary worker visa for him, we hadn't. He was therefore working for us—there was no other way of putting it—illegally. This was known amongst the band and crew, who made sure to keep it to themselves.

There was one item of personal information another member of the crew, a sound engineer called Rick, almost certainly wished he had kept to himself. This was his wife's habit of tucking a porno mag into his suitcase when he went away on tour, the idea being that it would keep him from going looking for female company in which to while away the nights after shows. We all thought this was very funny, including Johnette, who took it on herself to see that Rick didn't want for literature. Rick was duly inundated—magazines turning up not just in his suitcase, but in his hotel room, in the drawers of his bedside table, under his pillows. He decided that he oughtn't to let the favour go unreturned, and so Johnette began finding her own supply of material suited to her own inclinations. At one venue, she walked into her dressing room to find pictures of unclothed male bodies stuck up all around her mirror. I had checked the dressing room beforehand and found it devoid of pornography. Access to the dressing rooms being restricted to crew members, there was little question who had seen to the decorations. Though Johnette was hardly appreciative, this was within the bounds of acceptable japery, and so the pornography kept popping up. Rick, however, went and took things just that little bit too far...

Because ticket sales for Johnette's tour were fantastic and everyone was making a lot of money, the promoters were unusually accommodating, especially as our riders were quite modest. Were we sure we had everything we needed? Wasn't there anything else we would like? 'Well, actually,' I think Rick must have said to one of these promoters, drawing them inside, 'there is one thing, now that you mention it...'

For one evening Johnette was met by a discreet, and very obliging, promoter who presented her with a stack of male pornography, it being his understanding that this was something to which she was quite partial and trusting that it would meet with her satisfaction. Needless to say, Johnette was *not* amused, and immediately set about an elaborate scheme of retaliation.

We were staying in a hotel in New York. It was early morning and the sun wasn't up. Rick was sharing a room with the visa-less backline technician. They were woken by a knock on the door. Rick got out of bed and went to the peephole. Looking through, he saw a policeman stood out in the corridor. Rick's heart must have dropped into his bowels, for, in their suitcases, he and the technician were carrying small bags of something they shouldn't have been. He rushed back inside the room and told the technician to wake the fuck up, the fucking police were outside. The officer continued knocking on the door and asked them to open it. They scrabbled about in their suitcases for their stashes of coke and hurried through to the en-suite, shoved the bags in the toilet and frantically flushed them down. The technician jumped back into his bed and Rick went to answer the door.

'Good morning, officer.'

'Good morning. May I come in?'

'By all means, officer,' said Rick, coming over all obliging while he wiped the beading sweat from his brow.

The policeman stepped through to where the technician lay in his bed, peeping out from under his covers and making a show of blinking away sleep.

'How can we help you, officer?' said Rick.

The policeman looked over the room, its general untidiness rendering the mess they had made while retrieving their drugs relatively unremarkable. Though they had just lost a lot of money to the hotel's plumbing, there was at least no chance of the officer's finding anything.

'May I see your passports?' said the officer.

Rick nearly shit himself.

'Our passports?' he said.

'Um-hmm,' said the officer, hands on hips.

Rick looked over to the technician, who emerged from his bed and went to fetch his passport with its expired visa, then went to fetch his own. The officer stood before them, immaculate in his uniform, lips pursed, eyelashes beating beneath the brim of his cap. He held out his open hands and they surrendered their passports.

The officer's eyes held theirs, seeping guilt, then lowered them to examine their passports.

First he opened Rick's, and appeared to find everything in order. Then he opened the technician's. His eyes scanned the pages. He looked up at the quivering technician. Then he looked at Rick. And then he said:

'Hit it!'

There was a blare of sliding trombone and the officer flung the passports up into the air before flinging off his cap. Rick and the technician watched in disbelief as the officer proceeded to dance a striptease. At the appropriate moments in the song, the officer pulled off his shirt in one, then his trousers in one, and carried on dancing in his shoes, suspenders, socks and pouch.

Johnette, who had masterminded the whole thing, and had received the instruction to hit the play button on the CD player which she had brought out into the corridor, was doubled over with laughter. Rick and the technician, on the other hand, were rigid, still charged with fear in the expectation of the technician's imminent arrest and dismayed at having flushed all their drugs down the toilet for nothing.

I had been up since 5.30 that morning, having had a lot to do. As the lift doors opened, I heard 'The Stripper' drifting down to the landing. Following the music, I saw Johnette by the CD player, her nose near the floor. I strode down the corridor and entered the room to find the stripper down to his pouch and left sock. The hotel not being large, neither was the room, and so the performance was rather an intimate one. It didn't take much skill in face-reading to see that Rick and the technician were finding the joke thoroughly unfunny and that things were about to kick off.

First was to persuade the stripper to take his leave. I picked up his shirt and trousers from where they had landed while he continued dancing around me. 'Excuse me,' I said to him, 'but I think it's best if you wrapped up now.' Exhibitionist that he was, he was loathe to cut his act short. 'Johnette,' I said to the bobbing crown of Johnette's head. 'Johnette, turn the music off.' But for the flaring of their nostrils, Rick and the technician were statuesque in their lividity. 'Johnette, *please* turn the music off.'

The music stopped.

'Oh jeez,' said the stripper, as he let go of his left sock. 'Such a tough crowd.'

I handed him his clothes and asked if he wouldn't mind leaving. 'Whatever you say,' he said. 'Would you mind if I put my clothes on in the bathroom?' I said sure, go ahead. I watched Rick and the technician watching him as he sashayed to the en-suite with his bundled uniform.

Once the door clicked to, I asked what was wrong, thinking I knew full well about the business with the passports. Though I was ashamed to have been in on the joke, I didn't think it would help matters if they knew this, so I did my best to appear innocent and concerned.

Neither of them was able to come up with words: Rick was incensed, having lost his drugs; as was the technician, though he was still reeling from the prospect of a spell in a US prison. Johnette, meanwhile, was dying outside. I could see the morning's schedule going to pot if I didn't work quickly to placate the two men. I looked at them to tell them I was all ears.

'What's wrong,' Rick said eventually, his voice quiet with fury, 'is that we've just gone and flushed a shitload of very good shit down the toilet.'

This wasn't what I'd expected to hear. At this point I knew nothing about the drugs.

'You did *what*?' I said.

'We thought the stripper was a narcotics officer. We had some coke in our suitcases.'

'Just for personal recreation,' said the technician.

'And we flushed it down the toilet when Corporal Cupcake called.'

'Oh Kim,' said Johnette, staggering into the room. 'Oh, Kim, wasn't that magnificent?' She succumbed to further convulsions.

Rick's eyes daggered mine. 'You *knew*?'

I couldn't say I didn't.

'I don't believe it.'

'I didn't know about the drugs,' I said.

The bathroom door opened and the stripper stepped out, once more immaculate in his uniform, his cap on his head.

'Well I'll be seein' you crazies. Hope you enjoyed the show!'

Johnette assured him they did, they did, they most certainly did.

'Well *bless* you for saying that. At least *some*one is able to show a little appreciation.' He flicked a look at me, Rick and the technician, then, fluttering a hand, waved 'Bye bye!' and sashayed out into the corridor.

'If I'd known about the drugs, I could have done something about all this,' I said to the two men. 'Saved you flushing them down the toilet.'

'Yes, but we couldn't have let you know,' said Rick.

'You might have fired us,' said the technician.

'*Fired* you? I wouldn't have fired you. If it's for personal recreation and doesn't get in the way of the work, I haven't a problem with it. You should *see* what I've found in some of these people's suitcases,' I said, referring to the band and crew asleep along the corridor. I apologised for what had happened and suggested that we try and put it behind us, though it was really only the two guys who had anything to put behind them. It was going to be a while, I knew, before they were ready to think about forgiveness.

This incident marked the end of the escalation and put an end to all the pornographic provisioning.

*

The second story I have to tell about drugs disappearing down a toilet isn't nearly as funny. It happened during the summer of 1988, during Michael Jackson's *Bad* tour. I'd been looking for some work during that period and had been asked to supplement the merchandising teams that were travelling with the tour. Needless to say, Michael Jackson shifted a lot of merchandise. This meant for me, then, drafting about thirty sellers to go along to the gigs in Leeds and Liverpool and work underneath the employees of the tour's merchandising company. They would be put into teams, shown to a stand, given a quantity of stock, which they would count in beforehand. Then, at the end of the night, when they'd finished selling, they would count up the items of unsold stock and calculate how much money they had made before handing it over to the company's collectors.

I hadn't done this before and I hadn't worked with this company before either. I met with the three representatives to discuss the job and found that they were rather lacking in the charm department. Still, I agreed to do it, having no idea what a mistake this would prove to be.

The Leeds gig took place at Roundhay Park. The thirty sellers I had recruited were scattered around various tents. Four or five of them were to man a stall in a tent on the edge of the grounds near a small car park. They got set up and the show started. Given its remoteness to the stage, there were very few people about, and it wasn't likely to get much busier later in the evening.

At some point during the show, when it had gone dark, a gang of men opened up the back of the tent and stepped inside. They looked over the stock piled up behind the stalls and picked up four boxes of T-shirts, each worth about £1,000. The security man who had been stationed in the tent was nowhere in sight and wasn't seen again that evening. No one tried to stop the men; they looked the sort who wouldn't take kindly to obstruction. Thankfully, no one was hurt, only shaken up. Badly shaken up they were, though.

After the gig I went to meet the three representatives of the merchandising company to discuss what had happened. I was shown to a dinghy portacabin and asked to wait. I wouldn't have minded being kept waiting if it wasn't for five hours and I didn't have to catch a 7am flight to Geneva from London Heathrow and if I wasn't literally *kept* waiting. When the portacabin door was finally unlocked and the three men appeared, they told me I would be able to make up the loss—about £4,000—at the Liverpool gig the week after next and that we would be able to talk more about it then. I told them I'd wanted to talk about it five hours ago and that the only reason I wasn't going to talk about it then was that I had to catch a flight to Geneva, and so I left.

As there was no chance of us driving to London in time to catch the flight, my then husband and I drove to Leeds airport to see if we there was a flight to Heathrow we could catch which would enable us to make the 7am flight. There wasn't, and so we didn't get to Geneva that morning, which didn't make a bad day any better.

The week after next I was at Aintree Court with my recruits, who did all that was required of them. After the gig I met again with the three men. They told me I wasn't going to be paid. I didn't believe what I was hearing. Wasn't going to be paid? Did they think *I* was responsible for the loss of the merchandise? A gang of swarthy men had barged in and *stolen* it. I asked if they were joking, though I could see they weren't. 'You'd *better* pay me,' I said. 'I've thirty people I've hired who need paying for the work they've done. Some compensation for their ordeal wouldn't go amiss either.' They said that wasn't their responsibility. I said I knew it wasn't their responsibility—it was mine—but I'd only be able to pay them the money they were owed if *they* paid *me* the money *I* was owed. I'd done all that was asked of me; the theft of the merchandise was beyond my control. And just where the hell was the security guard who had been stationed in the tent? Making daisy chains?

After a while the discussion (much too dignified a work) broke down. I never was paid for the job. Since it was my responsibility to pay the sellers I'd hired for their work, I had to pay them out of my own pocket—about £4,000 in all. (Bear in mind that this was 1988.) Some of the sellers forewent their pay, others didn't and I don't blame them. In hindsight, I should have taken legal action, but at the time I was much too worked up and only wanted to forget about the whole thing. It was a truly horrible experience and I resolved never to work for another merchandising company off spec again.

It was only sometime later that I learnt that, shortly before the gig, the three merchandising men had been stopped by the police in their Winnebago and had had to flush all their coke down the toilet. They had a lost a lot of money—about £,4000. I don't have any doubts that they got it back, and that they did so by stealing merchandise from their own company—the cost of which, it just so happened, equalled the cost of the drugs they had lost. The gang of 'thieves' knew exactly what they were looking for and the T-shirts they stole were never recovered. I can't believe that it was a coincidence that the security guard had disappeared when they descended on the tent. The whole thing was a sham to recoup the money they had lost to their chemical toilet.

*

Those, then, are my two stories of drugs and toilets. The first has given me no end of amusement, the second I'd rather not have had to tell. I don't have any general objection to mixing business with pleasure, but it makes for a smoother combination when the pleasures are legal.

8

Violence, ultra- and casual

For many, rock 'n' roll is about more than the music; it's about indulgence, freedom, salvation. For others, it promises something rather less social: a chance for a fight. Rock shows are high-arousal affairs—the senses overwhelmed, the blood pumping, chemicals flowing (not all of them natural). It's not surprising that in such volatile conditions things tend to kick off. And then there's all the other things that go on off-stage—more chemical flow, all the money that changes hands, the sex and all the (possibly-related) human dramas. With all these cross-cutting interests, all these people wanting in on the scene, and the impulses to equality and restraint not being the most reliable in our species repertoire, it's no surprise that conflicts arise. And if reasoned argument doesn't suffice to get someone what they want, a fist or a gun might.

*

I'd been selling T-shirts at a Girlschool gig at Manchester Apollo and was driving down the M61, headed home to Hesketh Bank. It was late, dark, and pouring with rain. I could tell by the carking and clunking of the van's engine that something was amiss. I cajoled the van off the motorway and onto the slip road and juddered to a halt as the engine expired.

I sat with my hands on the steering wheel, the rain rattling on the roof, streaming down the windows, channelled by the windscreen wipers seized-up mid-swish, the noise of the motorway traffic washy and distant. 'Fuck,' I said. I turned the ignition key to see if anything would happen. Nothing did. What to do, I had no idea. I didn't know how to lift the bonnet, let alone fix whatever had gone wrong underneath it.

As luck would have it, I'd rolled up not far from a pub, and I could see a phone box in the distance. I leaned over and opened the glove box. I took out the hire documents and found a number for the AA. Change was one thing I wasn't short of. I opened the cash box sat on the passenger seat and grabbed a bag of 10ps. I closed the box and shoved the briefcase holding a carrier bag full of the night's takings under the passenger seat, covering the protruding end with

T-shirts. I zipped up my Rush tour jacket over my Girlschool sweatshirt and got out of the van, my trainered feet splashing in a shallow pothole and ran towards the phone box. I'd run halfway when I heard a vehicle behind me. A green estate car pulled up alongside. I stopped. The passenger window wound down, revealing a man with a black beard, the collar of his jacket turned up, a cap on his head.

'Stranded?' he said.

'Yes,' I said, gripping the collar of my jacket to stop the rain running down my neck. 'Van's broken down.'

'Terrible night for it.'

I wiped hair out of my eyes and said it was, hoping he was a do-gooder and that he'd hurry up about it if he was.

'You're wanting to use the phone box?'

I shook my bag of 10ps.

'It's out of order.'

'You're joking.'

'Afraid not. There's another up the road though. About a mile. I'll drive you if you like.'

I hesitated.

'Save you getting any wetter.'

'Thanks,' I nodded, stepping towards the car and opening the passenger door. I lowered myself into the passenger seat and apologised for getting it wet. I knew this probably wasn't what I should have done—getting into a solitary stranger's car on a dark night—but I really didn't fancy a walk.

As we drove, I began to think that either the man had seriously underestimated the distance or there was no phone box. I felt the weight of the coins in my hand and looked around for any sharp heavy objects when I saw the sickly yellow light of the phone box ahead. He pulled up and I got out of the van. I was waiting for someone to take my call when I saw the car reverse and head off back down the road. I was about to wave after him when my call was answered. I explained what had happened and roughly where I was and was told a mechanic would be on his way. I hung up and stood awhile in the shelter of the phone box.

Thanks a bunch, I thought. Surely he could have waited for me. And why had he gone back down the road when he had been coming up it before? In the reflective glass of the phone box, I could see what the rain had done to my make-up. I might have startled

Alice Cooper. At least I could feel more confident about my safety. I left the phone box and hurried back down the road. I hadn't gone far when a set of headlights appeared. The green estate pulled up. 'Sorry about that,' he said, through the passenger window. 'Had to go back for something.' He didn't say what and I didn't ask; I was just grateful I didn't have to walk the rest of the way. We drove back down the road and he pulled up a few metres from the van. I didn't see why he couldn't have taken me just that little bit further, not when he'd been as helpful as he had. I didn't say anything though. I thanked him and climbed out, apologising again about the seat.

I hurried over to the van and rooted around in my jacket pocket for my keys. Shit, I thought, reckoning I must have dropped them. I looked down at my feet, around the van, then along the road. Ahead of me the rear lights of the estate were receding into the rainy dark and panic flared as I thought my keys might be in it. There they were, though, in my pocket, with the 10ps. I stuck the key in the door and wiggled it about, desperate to get out of the rain, though I could hardly have got any wetter by then. I got the door open and brushed some powdery material off the front seat. I'd got most of it off when I realised that it was glass.

Glass?

It was then that I noticed my window was gone. I leaned in and looked under the passenger seat.

The briefcase was gone too.

In the front of the van I'd left a camera—not a bad one—along with two Sony Walkmans, which, not yet having been released in the UK, could have fetched a good price. Curiously, these hadn't been taken—the camera was where I'd left it on the dashboard, the Walkmans were in the footwell. The cash box hadn't been taken either. I went round to the back of the van, pulled open the rear doors and threw the bags of merchandise around, hoping I might find the briefcase somewhere amongst them.

I didn't.

I went back round to the front of the car, brushed off the rest of the glass and sat in the driver's seat, my breath quick as I thought of all that money I'd lost and however would I regain it. I don't know for how long I'd been sat there when I saw the lights of a police car in my rear-view mirror. I jumped out of the van and ran after it, shouting, waving my arms, wiping hair out of my face. A car coming up the road behind me, seeing me flailing, flashed its lights to attract the police car's attention. I saw the brake lights come on. The car reversed back down the road. I waved thanks to the other car. The police car pulled up and I stuck my head in at the driver's window, the officer flinching at the sight of me. Trying to recover my breath and not spit water all over his uniform, I explained what had happened—not all that well, his expression told me. When I got to the briefcase, he became more interested and rather less sympathetic.

'*How* much did you say was in this briefcase, miss?'

'I don't know. Not exactly. I'd say anywhere between four- and eight-thousand.'

'Between four- and eight-*thousand*?'

I thought he'd got his faces mixed up: the one he was wearing was for criminals, not victims.

'Could I see some identification, please?'

'Identification?' Oh shit, I thought. My passport and driving license were in the briefcase. Along with my Girlschool pass. I shook my head and said, 'No.'

'You refuse to present your identification?'

'I don't have it. It was in the briefcase.'

'In that case, I think you'd better come with me, miss.'

'Come with you where?'

'To the station.'

'The station? What for? I can't. I'm waiting for an AA mechanic to come and fix my van.'

'I'm not asking you,' he said.

'What about the van?'

'We'll call it in and have it taken to the station.'

'But what about the things *in* the van?'

'Don't worry about that. A patrol car will be along shortly.'

Slipping from panic into resignation, I got into the car. I didn't apologise for wetting the seat. 'Don't worry about the water,' he said, setting off down the road. 'There's been much worse on those seats.' Thanks for telling me, I thought.

We arrived at the police station. I knew I looked a mess but I didn't think the desk sergeants needed to look at me *quite* like that. If they hadn't got their criminal and victim faces mixed up, they were certainly short on sympathy. I supposed I couldn't blame them too much, looking as I did—as though I'd just been pulled out of a canal having fallen in under the influence of God knows what. I was taken through to a small brightly-lit room, the only pieces of furniture a wood-veneered table with a chair either side. On the table was a telephone, an ashtray and a box of tissues. I sat down and took some tissues to dab my eyes. I wanted to cry, but not in front of the officer. He struck me as a sadistic sort.

'The Inspector'll be in in a minute,' he said, backing out of the room.

I sat there and waited, piling up dirty tissues on the table. I had to remind myself that I hadn't done anything. I *was* the victim. The Inspector eventually came in and sat down opposite me. He said that he understood I was a merchandise seller. I nodded. He asked me who I was selling merchandise for. Girlschool, I told him. He raised his eyebrows. Even his face was square.

'You said there was between four- and eight-thousand pounds in the briefcase you claim was stolen.'

'I don't *claim*—it *was* stolen.'

'Well, you see, miss, this is where I'm having a little trouble. You say you had a briefcase containing a lot of money, you don't know how much exactly. You say that nothing else was stolen from the van. Not the camera or the Walkmans or the cash box or the merchandise—all of which might appeal to a thief. You say that this money came from selling merchandise. True as all this may be, we have no way of verifying it. We can't even verify who you are.'

'I've already told you—all my documents were in the briefcase! Where's the van?'

'Please don't raise your voice in here. The van's here, in our garage. We're just taking a look at it as we speak.'

I mumbled apologetically and took another tissue. The Inspector asked me if there was anyone I could call who might be able to verify who I was. My tour manager, Tom, I said. He asked if I had a telephone number. It was then I remembered that my address book had been in the briefcase too. That was a real blow—losing my address book—more upsetting than losing my other documents. There were addresses and telephone numbers of people I knew from way back; it would be a hell of a job getting them again—if I could get them at all. I told the Inspector I had no telephone number. He rolled his eyes had opened his mouth to say something asinine when I said I did know the name of the hotel where the band were staying. The Inspector didn't suppose I knew the number of the hotel. I didn't. He sent someone off to find out what it was. The number was dialled and I was given the phone. When hotel reception answered, I asked to be put through to Tom. I glanced at the Inspector while I waited, the receiver becoming slippery in my hand. Tom couldn't be found. In the end, Girlschool's bassist Ghislaine 'Gil' Weston was put on. I had got as far as telling her I was in Chorley Police Station when she interrupted me.

'Oh my God, Kim! What you have been done for?'

Her voice was appallingly audible over the phone.

'Gil, listen,' I said quietly, hoping she'd take a hint, 'I'm alright. Sort of. I was robbed. The merchandise money was stolen. The van broke down and while I was calling the AA someone broke into it and took the money.'

'You haven't got anything on you, have you?'

'I've been asked to provide identification,' I said, angling my head away, pressing the phone to my ear to try and stop her voice filtering out to the Inspector's. 'But that was in the briefcase too.'

'You *haven't* got a load on you, have you?'

This wasn't helpful. I asked to speak to Tom.

I heard Gil asking whoever she was with where Tom was.

'Tom's fucked off,' she said.

I asked if she could find him, stressing that I needed him to identify me to the police.

'Do my best. God, Kim, just don't let them find it!'

I slumped with relief when Gil got off the phone. The Inspector, if he hadn't heard every word, had heard enough. I kept the phone to my ear and waited for Tom to come on the line. After about ten minutes, he did. With a rush of relief, I explained to him what had happened. He said he would call management, they would sort it out. Hold tight, he told me. I'd try.

I relayed the conversation to the Inspector, who said he would step outside a minute. He was gone for rather more than a minute. When he returned, he looked even less amiable than he had before. He asked me how much money was in the briefcase. I told him again. 'Four- to eight-thousand pounds,' he said slowly. Would I say it was closer to four or to eight thousand pounds? he asked me. I told him I didn't know, the money had gone into a carrier bag to be counted up later. The Inspector said I must be deemed trustworthy. I told him not only was I deemed trustworthy, I *was* trustworthy. In the long course of the questioning, I mentioned I had recently bought a house. The Inspector's eyebrows went up. He asked if I had a mortgage. Yes, I had a mortgage. 'Four- to eight-thousand pounds would help with that, wouldn't it?' he said. I was astounded.

'Are you accusing me?' I said. 'Because if so—'

'Later,' said the Inspector. 'Now I'd like you to empty your pockets.'

'My pockets?'

'Your pockets.'

As it happened, Gil's worries weren't unfounded: in one pocket of my jacket I had a lump of dope, in the other, a gram of coke.

Okay…

I sat frozen while my brain sparked. Adrenaline carried me to a solution. I picked a crumpled tissue from the table and, pitifully as I could, I blew my nose. The tissue in my right hand, I stuck it in my right pocket, enveloped the dope in it, and pulled out the pocket—empty. Surreptitiously transferring the tissue to my left hand, I enveloped the bag of coke in it, and pulled out my left pocket—empty. Tissue in hand, I stood, unzipped my jacket and went through my other pockets. I sat back down and wiped my nose again, then put the tissue away. I was asked to submit to a breath test, which I did without hesitation, knowing I'd have no problem there.

I thought I might have been allowed to go but I was detained a good while longer and subjected to further questioning—about myself, the money, the stranger who had given me the lift to the phone box. The Inspector came right out and accused me of taking the money. I told him what I thought of that. I was released about 4am, the drugs in my damp tissue, and went home, distraught.

Later in the morning, having told my mum and grandparents what had happened, I called management. This was the scariest part of the ordeal—telling them I'd lost their money and not knowing how much exactly. I told them that the police had accused *me* of taking the money. I added that I hadn't. Management told me that they would get together with the police and the insurance company and would go from there. I put down the phone. The conversation had gone much better than I'd thought. My grandad, bless him, was livid. He went to Chorley Police Station, asked to speak to the Inspector and gave him a bollocking.

In the end, the police decided that I hadn't taken the money and the insurance company paid out. It transpired that mine was the third in a series of similar incidents. In each of the previous two cases, pairs of crew members had left Manchester Apollo after a gig and their vans had broken down on the road. In the first case, one of the guys had gone to call a breakdown service and returned to find the other beaten up beside the looted van. In the second case, the other guy had been beaten up *inside* the van. Both victims said they had been beaten with baseball bats. Petrol tests had revealed that sugar, or some sugary mixture, had been poured into the petrol tanks, and it was this that had caused the breakdowns. I was the only solitary target. I still shudder when I think how things might have turned out. It felt pretty hellish at the time but it might have been a hell of a lot worse.

*

There was another close call at a Girlschool gig—this one in Dundee. We were playing at a club and when we arrived we found that the venue was utterly unsuitable. We needed a stage of a certain size for all the equipment and props and it wasn't unusual to arrive at a venue and find that something wasn't right—the stage was made of blocks a foot high, say. In this case, however, *nothing* was right. We told the promoters they'd broken contract, we couldn't play the show.

The front doors were locked.

'You're playing,' the band were told.

They bloody well weren't, though. I was hanging around, waiting to get off, when I heard a crash and the sound of breaking glass. To me, that sounded like the discussion had broken down. Sure enough, this Dundee dive had become a Texan bar-room. Chairs and tables were being chucked and toppled, arms were being swung, glasses smashed. It was time to go.

I looked around for an exit. There was a long corridor, a fire exit at the end. I ran down it and heard running steps behind me— whose, I didn't know and I didn't look over my shoulder to find out. Reaching the door, I shoved the push bar and swung the door open, stumbling out into the night. I looked around and saw the other crew members behind me. 'Get in the fucking car!' someone shouted. We ran to the vehicles, fumbled with keys and dove in. The bus went past. I got into gear and lurched after it. In the rear-view mirror, I could see the promoters and club staff spilling out onto the car park, shouting and gesturing.

We stopped at a hotel—not the one we had been booked into. All of us had made it out. We checked in at this hotel, where there would be less chance of us and our vehicles being found, and holed up for the night. The Dundonian fans would have to be disappointed.

*

Weeks and months on the road—under pressure, sleep-deprived, confined to a tour bus or a hotel room—can put a real strain on relationships, even with the people you like, let alone the ones you don't.

Motörhead had just finished a tour of Europe. We were on the way back to London, and glad to be so. We travelled in two buses—the band in one, the crew in the other. The better of the two buses, needless to say, went to the band. They had to give it up at Calais, however, as it had been hired for another tour, which meant they would have to pile into the crew bus for the last leg of the journey across the Channel. This didn't seem such a bad situation, as we would hardly be on the bus, getting off once we were on the ferry and only getting back on in Dover for the journey to our hotels. The crew bus was smaller, though; it would be a squeeze. And that was just taking bodies into account, not personalities.

We arrived in Calais and the band refused to get off their bus. They were told they had to. The band wouldn't budge. They were told they didn't have a choice. The wrangling went on for God knows how long. At the end of it, the band were persuaded to get off the bus. They weren't happy, and had been drinking too, which didn't help. Moreover, it was a tighter squeeze than we had thought; there were people everywhere, flight cases, bags and boxes piled up and spilling out into the aisle.

No one was happy in the circumstances, but Phil 'Philthy Animal' Taylor had got really uptight. I'm talking seriously pissy. He was stomping up and down the bus with a look on his face that said: so much as look at me and I'll cut you. He had taken an acute, and quite inexplicable, dislike to one of the roadies, who everyone called 'Ratty'. Short of Phil having recognised Ratty from a past life in which Ratty had committed some unforgivable slight, no one could guess what he had against him.

Phil dropped into a chair and took a flick knife out of his pocket. He flicked the blade out and then folded it back, flicked it out, folded it back. He asked someone for their hand so he could play five finger fillet. They refused it. He asked someone else. They also refused. He threw the knife down in the table. By now people were starting to think perhaps someone should take the knife off him. Glancing up, Phil caught Ratty's eye.

'What are you looking at?' he said.

Ratty quickly averted his eyes.

'I said, what are you looking at?'

Ratty, edgy, shook his head and said, 'Nothing. Nothing.'

'Nothing, eh?' said Phil, managing to stand up. The knife in his hand, he stumbled up to Ratty. 'Didn't look like nothing,' he said, and belched.

'It was nothing,' said Ratty. 'Nothing.'

Phil thrust his sneering face right up to Ratty's. Ratty *was* looking kind of funny, his head turned to one side, his face screwed up, his nose wrinkled, trying to avoid the beery fumes. Phil flicked the blade.

'I'm gonna get you,' he said.

Ratty shrieked, stumbling back down the aisle as Phil lunged at him, bringing his hands up to his face.

The blade cut through the air as Phil fell forwards and landed in a heap on the floor.

'Jesus, Phil,' someone said, as people got hold of him. 'Get the bloody knife off him.' 'Is it bloody?' 'Don't know, where is it?' 'Where's the knife?'

'It's in my foot,' said Phil.

'Does it hurt?'

'No! It's in my fucking shoe!'

This burst the tension.

'He's stabbed his winklepicker,' someone chirped.

Phil yanked the blade out of his shoe and put a hand out behind him to steady himself. Those around helped him to his feet, while another took the knife out of his hand. 'Oi, give that back,' he said. No chance, he was told; he could have inflicted a very nasty wound. 'That's precisely what the fucker was asking for.' He lunged again towards Ratty, only this time he was held back. Someone told Ratty to get to the back of the bus. Ratty went. 'Come back you!' Phil shouted. 'I haven't finished with you! Get your hands off me!'

He tried to wriggle out of the arms of his restrainers, though he was too far gone to put up much of a fight. He snarled and said something unintelligible and was bundled to the lounge at the front of the bus.

Phil and Ratty kept well apart, the crossing went smoothly. At Dover, we got off the bus along with all our luggage to go through customs, after which we would get back on the bus and make the the drive to our hotels.

There was just one problem. Phil had disappeared. Completely.

His luggage was there, by the bus with everyone else's, but no one could find him or had any idea where he might have gone. None of us prepared to hang around, we took Phil's bags through customs, thinking he would probably turn up on the other side. He didn't. By this point, there was very little patience left between us. We got back on the bus and left the port. Phil could make his own way.

The next morning I got to the office. Phil's stuff was there, ready for him to collect. Doug Smith looked haggard. I asked what was wrong, and he told me. I wished he hadn't. There had been a stabbing not far from the offices in the early hours of the morning. You didn't need to be Sherlock Holmes to make the inference.

The next hours were passed making phone calls, preparing for the shitstorm and trying to work out what the hell the band was going to do while Phil submitted to criminal proceedings. Finally, however, he showed up. And most marvellously of all, he showed up twenty miles from the offices with a rock-solid alibi. There was no way he could have been responsible for the stabbing. That was it; the incident wasn't mentioned again.

All he'd hurt was his shoe.

*

Touring with a band is a great way of seeing the world. You don't have to go too far to realise what a lot of little worlds it's made up of, and how far apart these can be. Motörhead were playing Ljubljana, in what was then the Socialist Federal Republic of Yugoslavia. They were the first band to play there. We didn't know what to expect, though we had some ideas, and were not a little apprehensive. When we got there, however, we were treated like gods. Ask, and it would be done for us. My washing, for instance. I had two bags of dirty linen. I asked to have it cleaned. An hour-and-a-half after handing it over, I was presented with my linen, all beautifully laundered. I wouldn't have got that kind of service at the Plaza. No request was too great.

Apart from one, that is: a vegetarian meal. They seemed to lack the very concept.

Before the gig, dinner was served. Goulash. I explained that I didn't eat meat, could I please have something that didn't have any in it. With a funny look, I was told of course, and received a plate of rice with the sauce from the goulash along with some of the beans and vegetables carefully scooped out. I looked at my plate, then at the server and said I couldn't eat this—the sauce, beans and vegetables had been cooked *with* the meat, I might as well have eaten the meat too. I asked if I could please have something to eat which didn't have any meat in it *at all*. The server looked affronted. This suggested that the problem wasn't conceptual; there was something else going on. It looked like I would be going hungry until one of the crew offered a can of Heinz Baked Beans he had in his suitcase. He lived in Italy, where he couldn't get Heinz Baked

Beans, and, being partial, he would pick some up when he went on tour to take home with him. Gratefully, I accepted the offer, and ate a meal of rice and beans. Not the most luxurious of foods, but meat-free and filling.

The audience showed up for the gig, and were evidently excited, but we weren't selling any merchandise. People would come up to the stall and then turn away without buying anything, shaking their heads as they went. We were told that the merchandise was too expensive. We knew our merchandise was expensive, our profit margins were high, but fans always bought it because they wanted it. We hadn't considered, though, that these fans, members of a socialist state, had spent all their ready money on their tickets and simply hadn't any left over to spend on our over-priced merchandise.

Discontented by what must have struck them as flagrantly capitalistic displays of wealth, feelings didn't improve when Lemmy stopped playing halfway through the set. This must have seemed the ultimate in arrogance. The audience had paid all that money for their tickets and they were only going to get half a show. The reason he had stopped playing, however, was that he had been hit by a razor blade stuck between two coins thrown by someone in the audience.

The band got off the stage, the audience hissing and booing. We packed up and got out of there quick before things turned really nasty.

The food situation didn't improve. I hadn't eaten for three days. I was the only vegetarian on the tour and there was *nothing* for me to eat. Woozy and frustrated, I flipped—literally. (This was one of only three times in my career that I lost my temper.) Backstage, the caterers had laid out the food. There were two rows of three tables and another table at one end, forming a kind of horseshoe. I looked over the tables. As I had come to expect, there was nothing for me to eat. *Nothing*. So I turned over each of the tables in turn. I'd made a godawful mess and I thought it likely someone would notice.

Later that evening I grumbled to the promoter about my grumbling stomach. He looked at me, his eyes hard, and said there was one restaurant in a hotel he could have taken us to where we could have ordered a pizza. Well why the bloody hell hadn't he taken us there? He explained: at this upmarket hotel a meal cost a week's wages. He told us what a week's wage was. I didn't tell him that we often spent a lot more than that just on food. It was then that I understood the real difference in wealth and that meat was plentiful and cheap. It was very unpleasant, and must have been more so for him, our being able to afford what for most everybody else was prohibitively expensive. I needed to eat, but I made a point of being not nearly so shrill as I had been.

My table-turning, however, got the caterers' attention and the menu subsequently expanded.

*

Motörhead was also one of the first bands to go in to Catalonia. They were playing in San Sebastián and I was selling T-shirts in the foyer of the concert hall when I noticed security ushering people out. I wondered what they were doing. It was only a matter of moments before the foyer was clear of fans and about twenty Spanish guys strutted in. I was alone, with only a table and some T-shirts between me and them. The guys advanced, casual but dangerous-looking. They were talking loudly in Spanish. I had no idea what they were saying, though it sounded brash. I busied myself with the merchandise, trying to look as if I hadn't noticed them while watching their every move. Whoever they were, they didn't look like they wanted merchandise, and if they did, they didn't look like they'd be paying for it. They were quite close now, fanned out around the table. I couldn't call for help: security were the ones who had let them in.

It was then that I looked down into one of the boxes and noticed a bullet case. Motörhead were popular with the armed forces, and after one gig some ex-military guys had showed up with boxes of bullet casings. They were used to make bandoliers, which the band wore on stage. All the crew had been given one too. Not being all that wild about weaponry, I'd stuffed mine in a box of T-shirts. I shoved the T-shirts aside and there was my bandolier. I didn't know what the hell I was going to do with it but it looked pretty badass, so I grabbed it.

The Spanish guys halted.

Quite what made me think to do this, I don't know, but I wrapped the belt round my hand and slammed it down on the table. It made a hell of a noise. I didn't have a gun to show them, but there were quite a lot of boxes behind me, and if I'd just gone and pulled a full bullet belt out of one, I guessed they'd be given to wonder what I kept in the others.

The guys slowly edged away from the table, muttering uncertainly, and dispersed. Leaning forward on the table, gripping it to stop my arms shaking, I watched them go.

I hadn't been too impressed with Spain from what I'd seen of it. One of the reasons I had become a vegetarian was seeing a calf slaughtered in front of its mother for its steaks. This was not something I had ever seen before and I was struck by the brutality of it.

In Barcelona, Motörhead were playing at Real Madrid stadium. It is a testament to how the team has come on since the late '80s that their shower room was the dingiest I've ever come across. There was no chance of my setting bare foot on the tiled floor, so I had to go and buy some flip-flops before I could take a shower. During the show some members of the audience started throwing fireworks down into the merchandise stall. Amidst flashes and explosions, I asked a couple of guys to pack everything up. They did so, thankfully without injury. Whether this was another display of machismo or just plain mischief, I wasn't sure, only I knew it wasn't the sort of behaviour I was used to—and after all that time on the road, I'd got used to some pretty bad behaviour.

*

I had further experience of intimidation in Italy, though of a rather more organised sort. We were in Naples and rolled up at the venue. The door of the bus opened and the promoter (slim, dark, hair slicked back) got on. He told us we couldn't get off the bus. 'What do you mean,' someone at the front piped up, 'can't get off the bus?' 'You cannot get off the bus,' said the man. 'Not until you have handed over a box of T-shirts. Size extra-large.' Someone told him to fuck off. The promoter brushed off the insult and waited for us to comply. We quickly realised that until we gave him the T-shirts, he wasn't going anywhere, and neither were we. Better to give him the T-shirts. A box was too much, though, one of our guys said, initiating a process of negotiation, at the end of which it was agreed that we would give him twenty-five extra-large T-shirts and then we could get off the bus. One of us would have to get off the bus, though, to get the T-shirts from the hold. 'Who is responsible for the merchandise?' the man asked. That would be me. 'You,' he said, 'you may get off the bus to get the T-shirts.' I explained that I couldn't do it by myself, there was other luggage in the way that I wouldn't be able to lift. One of the roadies said he would assist me. The promoter nodded. 'Very well.' He let the two of us off the bus, we dug out a box of T-shirts, counted out twenty-five size extra-large and handed them over. He counted them and nodded satisfaction. 'You can get off the bus,' he said. 'Welcome to Naples.'

I had hoped that would be all the racketeering I was subject to for that day, but it seemed I was to be disappointed. Behind the merchandise stall later that evening, surrounded by half-a-dozen other stalls selling hot dogs, drinks, ice creams and suchlike, a group of well-groomed men strolled up who almost certainly meant business rather than pleasure. It was summer and it was hot, yet they wore full suits of exquisite tailoring, their collars crisp, the patent leather of their wholecut shoes gleaming. Over their shoulders were slung the most beautiful camel-hair coats. (It's the coats I remember most vividly. They were gorgeous.)

They approached the first stall in the ring and set a briefcase down on the counter. They reached into the till and took out a bundle of notes, counted them and put them in the briefcase. They went to the next stall and did the same. I had decided well before they got to me that they could help themselves to whatever they wanted, I wasn't going to stop them. I'd seen the *Godfather*. They approached my stall. I took a step away from the money box. Be my guest. They looked at me, looked over the stall, and returned their eyes to mine. They nodded, and went their way: I had paid already with the extra-large T-shirts, they weren't going to take any more. Sighing with relief, I watched them continue their rounds. They really were the most beautiful coats.

*

Organised crime is much less scary than its opposite. One time when I was with Rush working as a merchandiser, they were playing a gig in Newcastle. It was a sell-out gig, the place was packed, fans outside pressing to get in. Two guys had been caught climbing up a drainpipe trying to get in through an upper window. Shortly before the show as about to start, the promoter got a phone call. The caller didn't give his name, spoke with an Irish accent and said that there was a bomb in the building. (This was in the days when IRA bomb scares were commonplace.) Nowadays there would have been an immediate evacuation. In those days, however, things were rather different. The band were cleared out of the building and the dressing rooms and backstage areas swept for any suspicious-looking objects. When none was found, the promoter went out onstage and, quite calmly, asked if everyone could please stand up and look under their seats to see if there was anything underneath them and if there wasn't, could they please sit back down. There was a collective stirring as the audience got up, looked under their seats and when everyone was sat back down, the show went on.

Some years later, touring with Motörhead in southern Italy, we were driving overnight to the next venue when a black Volkswagen Golf started mucking about with us on the autostrada. This carried on for a while. We pulled in at a service station, as we usually did, to stretch our legs, get something to eat, brush our teeth. A group of us went in to the shop and I went off to the ladies, which was on the floor below down a set of tiled steps. There was no one else in there when I went in. I was in one of the cubicles when I heard the door swing open and two sets of footsteps enter. I heard one of the cubicle doors pushed open and smack against the cubicle wall. Then another, and another. My stomach tightened as I realised what was happening. My door was pushed. It didn't swing. Careful not to make a sound, I lowered to the floor and looked under the cubicle door. I saw two sets of boots. Mens' boots. Stood either side of the door.

Shit, I thought. Shit shit shit shit shit.

I had to get out of there. But how? I couldn't shout for help— I was too far from anyone to hear. I decided that my only chance was to try and make a break for it. I looked under the door again. There were the boots, either side. I edged away from the door and slowly unbent my knees almost to a sprint position. I reached out to the door lock, took a silent breath and turned it slowly. I took another breath and pulled open the door, springing out of the cubicle, keeping low to the ground. The men hadn't been expecting this and ran together. I had an image of them colliding into a clumsy embrace behind me. I stumbled to the floor, my arms out to break my fall and scrabbled on my hands and knees to the exit. I swung open the door, picked myself up and bounded up the steps. I could hear the men running up the stairs behind me. I felt the same fear I'd known as a child, playing chase, when you heard the chaser's feet falling behind you, running, running, just waiting for that moment when they caught up with you. Only here I knew the consequences of being caught would be much much worse.

I reached the top of the stairs and ran through to the shop. There they were, the crew. Some of them looked my way. The tour manager had his back to me and I ran and jumped onto it, sinking my head into his shoulder, wailing, tearful. 'Kim?' he said, swinging me round to see from what I'd been fleeing.

The men appeared in the shop and it all kicked off. To one side a café area had been roped off. The guys picked up the metal posts and started swinging these at the crew, hitting shelves, knocking goods onto the floor. Some other people in the shop joined the fray. Punches were thrown and received. I saw one of the shop staff run for a telephone. We managed to extract ourselves from the confusion of bodies, got back to the bus and piled inside. There was the Golf parked nearby. Sensing a definite imbalance in the scales of justice, one of the drivers thought to do something about it. By the time he was finished, there was an untidy pile of crumpled metal and broken glass. We got back onto the autostrada. It took me a long time to calm down but exhaustion helped. And with the morning, I felt much better.

9

Get Off of My Stage

For a time I was the tour manager for Chumbawamba. They were playing a festival gig. Though they weren't headlining—Bjork was—they were one of the main acts. Their dressing rooms were adjacent to Bjork's, which consisted of three portacabins. She also had her own personal security detail with her. The band were ready to go onstage and I was stood with them in the wings. Paul Greco was to play an introduction to the opening number on his harmonica. The musicians had started playing, it was almost time for Paul to go on and I noticed he wasn't there. He'd disappeared. The band were looking over, wondering where the hell he was. They continued with the introduction, drawing it out while they continued to throw bewildered glances into the wings.

I rushed down the steps at the side of the stage to try and find him. To my horror, I saw him in the distance, his head down, arms behind his back, being manhandled by security. I caught up with them and asked if they would please release him, he was supposed to be onstage. They said they had found him breaking into one of the dressing rooms. I looked to Paul, inviting an explanation. He told me what he said he had just told them—that he had left his harmonica in his dressing room (he pointed at the instrument in the hand of one of the security guys) and gone back to get it. Rather than faffing with a key, he climbed in through the window of the toilet which he knew to be open having left it open himself earlier on. Unfortunately for him, he had been spotted by the security guys, who had not unreasonably taken him for a burglar and waited outside the window so they could apprehend him when he climbed back out. Sure enough, they grabbed him and had been taking him off to ask him one or two questions when I saw them from over by the stage. If I'd been just moments later, they would have had him locked in a portacabin, probably roughed up a little, and reported him to the police. I would have had no way of finding him. As it was, I convinced them that he was who he said he was and persuaded them to let him go. 'Now go,' I said, and watched him leg it to the stage.

This wasn't the only emergency I had to deal with during my time with Chumbawamba. They were to play a gig at one of the Great Lakes. I couldn't believe the size of it; it was like looking out to sea. On the horizon we could see a storm gathering. It looked to be heading towards us. As we felt the first spots of rain, we knew we'd have to cancel the show, and set about unplugging all the equipment and taking everything down as the sparks started to fly. In a matter of moments it was lashing it down, the rain almost horizontal, swept onto the stage off the lake.

The band were going to play another festival in San Francisco. They said they needed a holiday and wanted to spend it in the city. It was thus arranged for everyone to stay on in San Francisco and do as they pleased, management paying for hotel accommodation and a per diem to each person to see them through. We were staying at the Fairmont hotel. The first morning of our mini break I walked into the marbled restaurant and found the crew in their shorts and flip-flops tucking into the breakfast buffet. At something like $30 a head, I wondered what our expense account would look like when the five days were over. I decided therefore that in addition to their per diem, everyone would get a food allowance.

At the end of the week we had to fly to Milwaukee for the next gig. The American Aviation Authority had recently introduced a rule that set a maximum weight of fifty pounds on items of luggage. We had all checked in at the airport and were about to board the plane when my name was announced over the tannoy. The others got on while I hurried off to see what the problem was. I was told that one of our items of luggage was too heavy; it would have to be split into two items. There was no way for us to do this and still make the flight. I needed a member of the crew to help me find the item and carry it around. We found the piece of luggage and the flight went. Taking it to the check-in desk, we stopped on the way to buy an extra case in one of the airport shops. We split the contents of the too-heavy item between the two cases and bought tickets for a flight to a destination a couple of hours' drive from the Milwaukee venue. All being well, we would make it in time. We got on the plane and arrived on schedule, taking a hire car to the venue. At the entrance we told security who we were and they waved us through. The place was rammed. There was no one to greet us. A police officer came forward to take us into the main area. As he led the way in and I heard the music coming from the stage, I stopped cold. I could hear Chumbawamba playing. I looked at my watch. They must have gone on early. And they didn't have the equipment we'd gone to all that trouble of getting there. We rushed to the stage, only to find that it *wasn't* Chumbawamba playing; it was a Chumbawamba tribute act.

These were some of my worst experiences of festivals, which only contributed to my general loathing of them. Alright for the band maybe, who are likely to be enjoying themselves on stage; alright for the fans too, listening to the band; but when you're stuck in a thin-walled office with a mass of paperwork to get through and not much time, with all that music and revelry as background, it's no fun at all. The most impossible conditions were provided by the German metal band Rammstein. The audience were making as much noise as the band—thrashing objects, starting fires. Not at all conducive.

Of all festivals, most hateful was Glastonbury. I've worked there twice. The reason for my so hating Glastonbury was the toilets. Nobody had warned me about them; I had no idea they would be so bad. Unusable, in fact. Thankfully, I was staying offsite, out in Wells, which was lovely, so I only had to worry about them during the day. I barely ate or drank a thing to ensure I didn't need to pay a call. The whole site was a mire; everything and everyone splashed with mud. There was no way I was going to venture out of our area to explore.

The second time I was at Glastonbury I was with Chumbawamba. Arriving at the site, we found that the main entrance had been blocked off: an extremely important person was due to enter the festival that way; all the other acts would have to use a secondary entrance. Following the directions we had been given, we drove over. The place was absolutely heaving—like Oxford Street on Christmas Eve. Eventually we got in, only we then had to drive over to the stage where Chumbawamba were to play. With all the chaos and the crowds, however, this was easier said than done. We ended up lost in Glastonbury.

One thing about the festival I did enjoy was looking out from the stage over the audience, out into the distance where the festivalgoers' tents stood out as little bright dots, flags fluttering above them. It was the same with other festivals. All those people descending on some godawful site out in the sticks to hear, if they couldn't quite see, the bands they loved.

*

In Los Angeles and New York, where the biggest gigs took place, celebrities would often show up while a band was playing. This could be quite distracting when they appeared in the wings while the band were onstage, so there tended to be strict rules about who was and wasn't allowed on the stage during a show. When Concrete Blonde had a gig in New York, only the monitor guy and the backline technicians and the band were allowed onstage. Security were told that they had to stand below the stage, at the sides, not in front of it. The band had gone on for an encore and I had gone off to my office to finish the ticket closures. While I was about this, I could hear a lot of noise coming from the direction of the stage. Moments later there was a knock on the door and one of the security guys walked in and told me they (security) had all walked off. I asked him what possible reason they could have had for doing that and hurried out after him.

It turned out that one of the security guys had stepped in front of the stage to make an imperious display in front of the audience, folding his muscled arms across his bright yellow T-shirt. Johnette had interrupted the song to ask him just what the hell he thought he was doing. The security guy must have been very embarrassed; he had wanted attention but certainly not that much. 'Look at this big fat fuck,' Johnette had said. 'Who the hell does he think he is? Just look at him, he's more fat than muscle.' She had then poured her drink over his head. 'There you go, jackass.' She might have been a rock star, but the security guy wasn't going to submit to this treatment. Between sweary blasts, he said he was going to sue.

This was bad. Possibly very bad. If he did file a lawsuit, Johnette's jibing could turn out to be very expensive. After the show, when everyone had had a chance to calm down, I met with the security guy, apologised for what had happened and asked him if there was anything I could do to make things right (i.e. to get him to not file a lawsuit). In the end we managed to agree on a restitution: we bought him a new shirt, had his clothes laundered and made him a gift of some Concrete Blonde T-shirts. The total cost was $400— quite a lot for a little (albeit very public) abuse and a wet T-shirt but certainly a *lot* less than a settlement reached in court. Thenceforth, Concrete Blonde took their own T-shirts for security to wear at their shows—a lot less garish than the bright yellow ones from the New York gig.

*

Sometimes it's other bands that need keeping offstage.
Talking Heads turned up one night to hear Concrete Blonde play.
They came backstage and were received by the band straight after
the show, which was unusual since bands normally like to take
fifteen or twenty minutes to recuperate after they've come off. They
said how much they had enjoyed the show and David Byrne said that
the band should have played a certain number, I forget which. The
band said they would play it then. Reluctant as I was to be a wet
blanket, I told them that would not be possible as the equipment had
been packed away.

There was a round of ah-wells and another-times and it
seemed that that would be that until one of the Talking Heads
suggested that the crew unpack the equipment and set it up again,
surely it wouldn't be *too* much hassle. Having taken on the wet
blanket role, I got deeper into the part and told them that it would in
fact be too much hassle, the crew wouldn't be happy, there were

contractual expectations, and so forth. 'Oh I bet they wouldn't mind,' said David Byrne. 'Why don't you ask them?'

I noticed with dismay that Concrete Blonde's post-show fatigue was beginning to wear off. They started talking about the song, the Talking Heads egging them on to play it while Concrete Blonde became itchier to go out and do so. 'The crew would *love* it,' said David Byrne. I thought this was doubtful. They would all be jiggered and looking forward to getting back to the hotel to have something to eat and drink. There wasn't much more egging-on before the band decided to go back out on to the stage. They asked the crew if they wouldn't mind unpacking the equipment and setting it up again so they could play a number for the Talking Heads, who were standing off to one side. There were some huffs and eye-rolls and your-fucking-kiddings but the good and faithful crew acquiesced and started unpacking everything for the second time that evening. There was quite a lot of audience members still in the bar. Because Concrete Blonde often changed their set, their audiences were always reluctant to leave. They therefore had a pleasant surprise when they heard the noises coming from the stage as the instruments were plugged back in, and made their way back through to the auditorium, drinks in hand. The band picked up their plectrums and drumsticks and played a special impromptu performance for the Talking Heads and those audience members who hadn't had to hurry home. Pain that it was, I don't think the crew did mind too much in the end, and back at the hotel they were bought drinks by the band as a thank you.

There was more drama with Concrete Blonde when they were joint headliners of a big outdoor gig with Joan Jett. The problem with having a double headliner is that both bands can't finish the show. Concrete Blonde weren't that bothered and so ended up going on first. We travelled overnight, arriving at the hotel in time to get to the venue later that afternoon. When we went into the dressing room we found a huge ice sculpture of a crab surrounded by all kinds of seafood—crab, lobster, oysters. Johnette asked what the hell it was doing there. The promoter said that it was a present. Johnette said to get it out of there. Dismayed, the promoter asked for the melting decapod to be removed. It took eight people to shift it.

We settled in and then went to get set up, only to find that the stage was already set up for Joan Jett. I went onstage and introduced myself to the band and crew, asking if they wouldn't mind leaving the stage, I presumed they'd finished their sound checks. They exchanged glances, saying they weren't quite ready. They said there'd been a delay, Joan was having some trouble with hair dye, they couldn't do the sound checks until she was ready. I said she'd better hurry up, people would be arriving soon. They said they were sorry but nothing to be done, their tour manager had been looking for me. (Actually he'd been avoiding me; if he'd wanted to find me, he knew where to look.) I asked if they couldn't just move their equipment, then we could get set up and do our checks. They said that wasn't possible, everything was plugged in, the drum riser was fixed in position. Not having any time for silly buggers, I walked across the stage and surreptitiously took the brakes off the riser before sitting down on the edge of it. 'Surely, it's not *impossible*,' I said, and casually rolled the drum riser back with my feet. Grudgingly admitting that they might be able to reposition some of the equipment, they set about it and Concrete Blonde came onstage, set up and did their checks, all before the doors opened.

*

My worst experience of getting a stage ready was in Italy during the time I was working with Motörhead. There was one summer when their road crew didn't have any work on. A couple of the guys lived in Italy, one of whom was Dil, the monitoring engineer, and they had decided to fill the empty summer months by going on tour with the Italian singer Fiorella Mannoia. Italian road crews were notoriously laid-back and a British contingent was wanted to keep things on schedule. Not having any work to do either, I decided to join the tour too, and flew out to Pisa, where I met Dil, who invited me to stay at his villa which was just quarter-of-an-hour outside the city. I found after I arrived that the villa didn't in fact belong to Dil but to the drummer and founding member of Cream Ginger Baker. The villa sat atop a hill, surrounded by an olive grove and vineyard. The only place to eat was a trattoria at the bottom of the hill, about a mile's walk. You'd walk down, get pizza and get drunk so as to make the walk back up the hill less unbearable. At the top, Ginger would be ready to restore us with more red wine. He bought it by the barrel (something like £2 per) from some monks who lived in the hills close by.

One of Fiorella's performances was to take place in some stunning gardens, stone steps leading down to a private beach, the sea warm and blue beyond. We had been there half-an-hour when it got to twelve o'clock and someone called lunch. No one had done anything. The stage wasn't built, no equipment had been unpacked. There was extra pressure to get everything done because the show was to be televised. Disbelieving, I sat down to lunch.

Four hours later, after a heavy meal and copious quantities of red wine, we started pushing ourselves up from the table, a few others having gone for a swim. Everyone was drunk. There was no way we were going to be ready on time. And we weren't. I hadn't gone five yards from the long table strewn with the remnants of lunch when I lost the keys to the minibus which I'd been entrusted with. I knew I'd had them when I sat down but couldn't for the life of me think where they might have got to. In the end we had to break in to the minibus and hot-wire it to take it to the next gig. 'Later, later,' was the constant refrain as the sun went down and the stage didn't go up. That's how we referred to Italian crews: 'Later', or 'Tomorrow'. Fiorella went onstage at 4 am—eight hours later than she should have done. The glamorous audience, who had gone to extra trouble to look their best knowing they were to be on television, had lost a little of their sparkle by the time they took their seats.

The next five days were the same: people turning up shortly before noon, just in time for a long boozy lunch, the stage constructed with maddening leisure throughout the evening, Fiorella stepping out in the not-so-early hours of the morning. It was totally silly. The Italians, I thought, were well able to work behind schedule without us Brits, so I decided I'd had enough and left the tour at Rome, flying back to England.

*

Showbusiness is unpredictable. Some gigs come off, others don't. Once, at a festival in Scandinavia, a barrier collapsed and a member of the audience was tragically killed. Chumbawamba were due to go onstage. They said they weren't going to. The promoter's tried to persuade them but they were resolute. A man's just died, they said; we're not playing.

One of the gigs I really regret not happening was Chumbawamba appearing at the opening ceremony of the Paralympic Games in the States. Eunice Kennedy was the organiser and asked the band if they would perform 'Tubthumping', an apt choice. The band declined, their reason being that they had just come off tour and had all booked much-needed holidays. They had discussed the matter at their fortnightly meeting and this was the decision they'd come to. It was shortly after they gave their reply that Eunice Kennedy wrote me a beautiful letter asking if I might ask them to reconsider. It was with great disappointment that I had to write back that it was up to the band and they had made their decision, there was nothing I could do.

Another gig Chumbawamba didn't play was T in the Park. This time, however, it wasn't down to them. They were on a tight schedule, having flown into Heathrow from Reykjavik and caught the shuttle up to Glasgow, from where they were to fly by helicopter to the festival. High winds, however, made the helicopter ride impossible; they would have to travel by car. Their equipment would follow in a van. We had been careful to make sure the equipment got from Heathrow to Glasgow but when we arrived we found a keyboard was missing. They *had* to have this keyboard since it was specially programmed for their set. I complained to a representative of British Airways. The band were to play a daytime slot and at festivals timing is crucial. BA managed to locate the keyboard and said they would have it flown up to Glasgow and driven to the festival. We arrived at the festival and got set up and waited for the keyboard to arrive. It was time for the band to go on and it still wasn't there. In the end the band went onstage and said to the audience they were sorry, they wouldn't be able to play, they didn't have all their equipment, blame British Airways. They weren't going to hang around as they had spent £10,000 on a plane to fly them from Glasgow to Leeds so they could get home in time to watch the World Cup, so off they went, leaving a disappointed audience. The keyboard turned up one-and-a-half hours later. I told the driver it was too late, the band had left, they hadn't been able to play. I asked him what had happened. It turned out that, having been given free admission to the festival, he'd stopped off en route to pick up a friend he thought would like to go along too. If he hadn't made the stop, he would have been on time.

Of all the missed opportunities, there's one I can't quite believe: the time Credit to the Nation turned down Nelson Mandela's invitation to perform for him. Mandela had heard about these bright rap artists from Wednesbury, whose lyrics were powerful and morally engaged. I still don't quite know why they turned Mandela down. Perhaps it was to make a statement, perhaps it was nerves. I tried to persuade them to reconsider but to no avail.

It so happened that the gig which gave me the greatest pleasure was the one for which I was least prepared and which had been arranged last-minute. That day, everything that could have gone wrong had gone wrong. I had been in press interviews all day with Concrete Blonde and pestered by record company personnel and journalists wanting to be added to the guest-list. Johnette had been asked to go and sing the American national anthem before a basketball game. It would be just me and her going and would take 30-45 minutes, the stadium just being a short drive from the venue for that night's concert. A limousine was sent to collect us and we were driven inside the stadium through the VIP entrance. We were escorted to a dressing room filled with every sort of refreshment we might have wanted, a steward stationed outside the door to fetch anything that might have been omitted. We were only going to be there for quarter-of-an-hour. We had a look over the sagging tables and then it was time for Johnette to go out. We were led through to the court and she walked on in her heeled shoes—which she shouldn't have done (only specially-approved trainers being permitted on court).

Whenever anyone does a rendition of the national anthem, they try and put their own spin on it. Johnette, with no accompaniment, just her voice, didn't disappoint, holding a note here, dropping one there. It didn't sound great to me, a little warbly, but it was an affecting performance. At the end of it everyone went wild. Johentte left the court and we returned to the dressing room, where we had to stay until the players went out. The door was opened and we were told we could leave. We got in the limo and were driven back to the venue, which was in a state of utter chaos, the doors having opened three minutes before. The guest-list wasn't on the door, it had to be downloaded from the computer. (This was in the days of dial-up internet.) Record company personnel were jostling outside, insisting they were on the guest-list, and had to be told to wait. It was utter pandemonium. A gig to forget. But that brief interlude at the stadium I'll always remember and, of the many privileged moments in my career, is the one I feel most privileged to have been a part of.

*

It was shortly after the troublesome New York gig that Concrete Blonde played the Wiltern Theatre in Los Angeles. Given what had happened in New York, we were even more alert to make sure there was no one on or around the stage who shouldn't have been. As I mentioned earlier, the reason for this wasn't so much safety; it was ensuring that the band weren't distracted while they were performing. Big city gigs are always the most nerve-racking, since it's those gigs their artistic peers are most likely to go to, the major critics too. We had an intern on the doors with the guest-list. Guest-lists are always very particular—artists don't want just anyone rich and famous coming backstage to say hello, so only some guests will get to go backstage, others will get front-of-house treatment, while others will just get a ticket to the show. Promoters don't like to give away tickets, so guest lists are always strictly adhered to. Once, at the Viper Room in West Hollywood, which was then part-owned by Johnny Depp, I was tour-managing a band and had gone out of the building without taking my pass with me. When I tried to get back in, security wouldn't let me. Upon admission, guests had to pay $20 to charity. Not having $20 on me, I had to borrow it in order to get back in.

Before the gig, I was looking over the Wiltern's stage when I noticed a woman stood in the wings. She had blonde hair, parted down the centre with clips at the side, and was wearing a plain mauve T-shirt and no make-up. I strode over to her. The monitor guy, sensing my purpose, was waving his arms at me, his eyes wide and mouthing 'No'. I knew she wouldn't be a complete nobody and had assumed she was a girlfriend of some big name. Still, she shouldn't have been there. Ignoring the monitor guy's warning, I told her so and asked her could she please leave the stage. 'Oh, sorry, sure,' she said. 'I didn't realise I wasn't supposed to be here.' She descended the steps and walked off.

'You *do* know who that was?' said the monitor guy. 'No,' I said, 'and frankly I don't care. She shouldn't have been here.' Curiosity prevailing, however, I said, 'Go on, who was she?' He stared at me a moment before replying: 'Madonna.' I admit I did quiver a little when he said this. I brought to mind the image of her: hair clipped and parted, mauve T-shirt, no make-up. She hadn't looked like Madonna, and though I could see now that it was her, I had the small consolation that I could be forgiven for not recognising her. Even if I had, though, I reflected, I would have still asked her to leave. Though perhaps a little less tersely.

She hadn't made any scene then and she didn't make a scene afterwards. Of course she didn't. She knew that if she was in the reverse situation, she wouldn't have wanted anyone hanging around the stage to distract her during a performance. She had only been sweet and apologetic, entirely understanding. I might have hoped I'd meet her in different circumstances—circumstances in which I was at least aware I was meeting her—but I wasn't too dejected to say I'd just thrown her offstage. She had been professional and good-natured and I was happy to keep my memory of that brief encounter. I didn't know then that I would meet her again. At least, I think I did.

10

Bands Behaving Badly

Rock bands aren't known for their good behavior and they're invariably worse on tour. Often, as with Motörhead, misbehaviour is simply a response to boredom. All the travelling, the waiting around, being told what to do, where to be, when to be there, punctuated by the rush of performance—it's both tough and tedious.

Understandable as it may be, however, bad behaviour can make a tour manager's job a whole lot harder. Tours don't just happen and, when everything has been so precisely arranged, it doesn't take much to stop them happening at all.

*

Chumbawamba were to appear at a festival in Iceland. Flying from Heathrow, a lot of the other festival acts were on the plane with us. When I was flying with a band, normally I would sit behind them to make sure they were alright, that they didn't get in trouble with the airline staff, that they got the meals they had requested, and so forth. Meals were a great source of trouble. Band members would make ludicrously outlandish requests which were almost guaranteed not to be met just for the hell of it. If they didn't get what they asked for, they would kick off, and it would be my job to placate them and see what nearest approximation the airline staff could rustle up. On this flight, however, I wasn't able to sit behind Chumbawamba. Instead, I ended up at the back of the plane sat next to Ian Brown. Given his reputation, the band were delighted with this and they would walk past on their way to the toilet to see what Ian Brown was up to. For one, he couldn't keep still. He would be drumming on his knees, patting his pockets, shifting about, standing up. 'Please sit down, Mr Brown,' an attendant would say. And it started all over again. For all my apprehensions, however, I found him delightful company and very charming.

We landed in Iceland and got to our hotel, from which a coach would collect us the following morning to take us all to the festival venue. As was most everybody else, I was anticipating that we would be late setting off and that it would be Ian Brown who would be responsible. We had joked at Heathrow that the flight would be delayed because of him. Ian hadn't delayed the flight and he didn't delay the coach the next morning. We shared surprised glances as he walked out of the hotel and got on the coach. Not only was he on time, he was early. The other acts came out in dribs and drabs and at last we were all ready to leave but for a horn player from Chumbawamba's brass section. He had woken, I knew—I'd given him his wake-up call. From the lobby, I called his room to ask him where he was and he told me he was in his room. I told him I knew he was in his room and to hurry up and come down, we were very nearly late. He didn't come down. I went up to his room and knocked on the door. Eventually he answered it. After I'd called him, he'd gone back to sleep. I told him to get dressed and get down to the coach. He did, and we left for the venue. Late. But not because of Ian Brown.

This horn player caused more trouble when Chumbawamba were in Portugal for another festival, though this time he wasn't really to blame. The morning after the gig the band were scheduled to return to London on a 07.10 flight with British Airways. This would allow the horn player to get to a gig in Leeds that he was due to play that night. When we got back from the festival, I asked the promoter who had booked the plane tickets what time we would be picked up in the morning from our hotel. He said we did not have to leave till the afternoon, we could have a lie-in, a leisurely lunch, we would not have to leave till five-fifteen. Plenty of time. No, I said, our flight was at seven-ten. Yes, said the promoter. He looked at me as if I was unhinged and I did likewise. I asked him to please tell me he wasn't operating on a 12-hour clock. He was. He had booked us on an evening flight. This was frustrating but it didn't seem like it would be too much of a problem: it was only the horn player who had to be back that night; as long as he got on an earlier flight, the band could take the later one and no real harm would be done. When the band found out, however, they went ballistic. The suggestion of another day in Portugal (lie in, leisurely lunch) didn't meet with approval. Suddenly everyone had something they urgently needed to get back to England for. I looked forward to a long night not sleeping.

I called British Airways, explained what had happened and asked if I could have the seventeen tickets for the 19.10 flight that had been booked for the band and crew changed for tickets for an earlier flight. *How* many tickets did I want changed? Seventeen, I said. Doubtful noises came through the receiver. I called management to ask them to weigh in. They did so, and in the early hours of the morning I received confirmation that we would all be able to take an earlier flight, nothing extra to pay. Another instance of what a little stardust can get you. No doubt it had helped that this was during the French World Cup, when 'Tubthumping' had been chosen as the anthem of the tournament and had consequently been heard continuously for weeks—a great boon for the band. As I lay down to snatch what little sleep I could before the flight, I tried to forget that, but for the horn player, no one else had actually *needed* to get back that night. When you're famous, you can get things you want that you really don't need which Joe Bloggs wouldn't even dream of.

This wasn't the only time I had trouble with Chumbawamba catching a plane. We were in Copenhagen, where Chumbawamba had played a festival gig, and were going on to another in Germany. They had a huge entourage with them. At our hotel that morning, where the checking-in and -out process had just been computerised and each person needed their own invoice, it had taken nine hours to check out. Despite this delay, we were okay for time. The airport was only about thirteen miles away. By the time we got there we could see a number of other the festival acts waiting to check-in, many of them bound for the German festival. With all these famous faces among the many waiting, the staff were pretty ruffled. Eventually I got to the desk and put all the tickets and passports on top and we started putting the luggage (numbered according to a special system so we could keep track of each item) onto the conveyor belt. It was with horror that I watched as the woman serving me, getting increasingly flustered, knocked the tickets off the desk onto the conveyor belt. I made a vain grab for them before they slipped underneath the belt. The woman apologised. I made a vague gesture of acceptance though my thoughts were far from forgiving. She picked up a phone and put a call through to the engineers. While we waited, I sent everyone whose documents hadn't gone under the conveyor belt ahead to catch the flight, giving them the luggage notes I'd made so they would know which bags they were to collect at the other end. The engineers took twenty-five minutes to arrive. By the time they had retrieved the documents, the flight had gone. I asked the woman, from whom apologies and admissions of responsibility had been flowing unceasingly, to see her supervisor. It turned out that he had been present and seen all that had been going on. First he apologised, then he said: 'Kim, my name's Kim. I'm therefore going to help you.' He got the rest of us onto another flight which landed at a different airport, nearer to the festival venue, so that in the end we arrived before everyone else.

Another time it wasn't airport staff who were to blame. Chumbawamba had just finished a tour of Europe and were flying back to London via Brussels. Having checked in, Boff Whalley and one of the crew went off to a champagne bar and both got drunk as lords. Our flight was called and we prepared to make our way to the gate. It was then that Boff and the crew member realised that they didn't have their passports. I had given their passports to them on the tour bus earlier on and they had to have brought them into the airport else they wouldn't have got in. They were making a second round of pocket-patting and bag-checking when I told them they *had* to find them or we'd miss the flight. Wherever they were, they couldn't find them.

Through all the years travelling, I had accumulated a detailed knowledge of the layouts of literally hundreds of airports—which cafés were in which departures lounges, which perfumeries, which restaurants, where the toilets were. I knew where there was a record store in the Brussels airport and hurried over there. I found a selection of Chumbawamba albums and bought one which I knew had a picture of Boff in the CD booklet. I found Boff and the crew member making another desperate round of pocket-patting and took them to the customs desk. I explained to the officer that the two sauced, though quickly sobering, men with me had lost their passports, that they were, respectively, members of the band and crew that I was responsible for, which responsibility I could prove with various items of paperwork, and that this gentleman here (indicating Boff) was the very same as Boff Whalley here pictured in this CD booklet, this other gentleman (indicating the crew member) I had no way of identifying other than saying he is who I say he is. I asked if an exception might be made for them on this one occasion so they could pass through and make their flight which they really couldn't miss. I used a lot of 'please's.

The officer, to my utter relief, said that he was prepared to make an exception in this case, although (leaning in close to my ear) they would have a bit of fun first. He called Boff forward and, after looking him over and telling him he really oughtn't to be doing this, allowed him through, Boff spouting gratitude as he went. The officer called the crew member forward. He looked him over and asked him to please step to one side. Now quite sober, the crew member submitted to the officer's scrutiny. The officer said he would have to search him and was about to do so when he cracked up. The crew member paled confusedly. The officer explained that he was joking, only joking, he could go through. Flushed and jittery, the crew member thanked the officer and went through. After that I started carrying out my own passport checks.

This was just one of the times I had to fork out to save the band. Another was when the band had a festival gig and Boff had thrown up in the artists' bus which shuttled the acts between the venue and their hotels. We were already in the driver's bad books after he dropped us off at the venue earlier in the day only for Danbert Nobacon to realise that he had left his stage clothes back at the hotel, which meant the driver taking me back to collect them and then back to the venue in a mad rush. At the end of the night, I gave him a very large bonus in compensation.

Exasperating as this had been, I think it was probably less so than the time the band wanted to go and say hello to the Pogues' Shane MacGowan, who was at the festival where they had just finished a show. The guys had been drinking, as had Shane, and to the same heroic extent. Their saying hello turned into a one-and-a-half-hour conversation, the winding, looping course of which, being sober, I found completely impossible to follow. They kept falling off their stools. Thinking that one of them was going to end up in the fire, I sat poised throughout to rescue them from the flames.

*

Chumbawamba had a habit of getting into trouble. There was a lot of them in the band and as they often brought their friends there was plenty of egging-on. But whether they deserved the trouble they got into was often a matter of ideological inclination. If you were anarchic, leftist or libertarian, most likely you'd commend their antics, which were often motivated by their political and philosophical views, and not mere hooliganism.

One of the things they really disliked was schmoozing. Record companies are always looking to take bands out for meals at excellent restaurants to discuss potential moneymakers. The guys simply had no interest in this oily mechanism. It was thus a rare occasion when we all went out for a meal with about twenty people from Universal at a Turkish restaurant in New York. The band and crew making up a similar number, it was a big party. The new smoking laws had just been introduced and so people kept getting up to go outside and squeeze into the smoking area for a cigarette. The meals would be brought out from the kitchen and whosever it was wouldn't be there. Some were sat waiting for their food while meals were going cold at empty places. There wasn't one moment when everyone was sat at the table together. At one point there were more people outside than in. Just getting us all there had been something of a palaver: almost an hour had passed between the first taxi's arrival at the restaurant and the last's. We certainly wouldn't be doing it again anytime soon.

Given the band's leftist views, it was with some surprise that, while I was with them in northern Italy, I heard a garlicky communist tell me that come the revolution I'd be first up against the wall. 'Excuse me?' I said. He told me again, slower this time: 'Come the revolution, you will be first up against the wall.' I told him I didn't know what I'd done to earn that distinction. He told me I was in the service of capitalist regimes and that when the revolution came and the capitalist pigs were overthrown, no mercy would be shown. He added that if I let him and his comrades in—two-hundred of them, he said there was—I might be spared. I told him no way. 'Come the revolution—' I cut him off and said, 'Come the revolution, I won't be here.'

Later on the tour, the band were to play a festival in the Italian countryside and we were staying at a hotel in a small town close by. Dunstan Bruce and one of the backline technicians, unappreciative of the Gideons' evangelicalism, decided that they would purge the hotel of its Bibles. The unoccupied rooms not being locked, they went through them and collected all the Bibles and chucked them out of a window into the piazza. It wasn't long before a flock of pious townsfolk—most of them slight, stern, black-clad women—were making vocal protest at this terrible profanity, banging on the doors of the hotel and calling for the expulsion of the godless guests. Looking out into the piazza from Dunstan's window, I envisioned a lynching.

The hotel manager duly appeared along with the Italian promoter. Torn between his responsibilities to his business and his Lord, the manager said it was a most upsetting thing they had done.

Egregious, said the promoter. I said there had been a most unfortunate misunderstanding, glancing at Dunstan and the technician to signal that I would do the talking. They had not meant to throw the Bibles out of the window, I said. 'Then how do they end up in a pile in the piazza?' said the promoter. Fumblingly at first, then with greater assurance, I said that Dunstan and the technician, good-natured men both and neither hostile to Christianity, had found a box in one of the cupboards and, deciding that it didn't belong there, had chucked it out of the window, not realising that it was full of Bibles. Admittedly, they shouldn't have done this, they should have informed one of the hotel staff and asked them to remove the box for them. The manager nodded. If they had known the box was full of Bibles, however, they wouldn't have dreamed of throwing it out of the window, I said. The manager bought it and so did the promoter. I was about to suggest that Dunstan and the technician go and pick up the Bibles when I saw that the townsfolk had already done this for them.

To be fair, not all the trouble Chumbawamba got caught up in was down to them. One night after a festival show in Germany we had to drive to the airport to drop off one of the crew members before the rest of us went back to our hotel. What should have been a twenty-minute drive turned into the most circuitous three-hour crawl around the city. The reason for the disruption to the roads: Marilyn Manson had gone onstage after us that night and had started a riot. Eventually, having dropped off the crew member in time to catch his flight, we went over to the Hilton Munich Airport, a stunning building with its amazing glass foyer. I'd have loved to have spent more time there. As it was, I think it was the shortest stay I've ever experienced. I checked everyone in and they went up to their rooms, went up to my room, had a quick look around, and it was time to check everyone out again.

For all their playing up, Chumbawamba did a lot of good. Every fortnight, before they took their money out, they would sit down and sift through communications from unfortunate people who'd lost their jobs, been evicted, were struggling to pay the bills, and give significant chunks of their earnings to those they decided needed it the most. The 1997 election had been a great disappointment. Like many Labourites, they saw that Tony Blair had sold out.

It was at the Brit Awards the following year that Danbert Nobacon was accused of jumping on John Prescott's table and tipping an ice bucket over his head. The incident was reported in all the papers. Prescott was livid and thought it 'utterly contemptible that his wife and other womenfolk should have been subjected to such terrifying behaviour,' according to a statement from his office. I say 'accused of' when in actual fact he took the rap for one of the band's entourage. I got a call at quarter-past-two the following morning from the band's manager asking me to get on a plane to London. I wasn't the band's tour manager at the time and was out of the country on a trouble-shooting assignment. The tour manager was quite upset, having tried to handle the situation by apologising to the press on behalf of the band. The band weren't at all happy about this as they had no intention of apologising—they thought it was terrific! Even a private apology would have been out of the question— perhaps more so than a public one. The best response for her to have made would have been to express her personal disapproval of the incident while acknowledging that the band might not feel the same way. This would have meant that the band could capitalise on the attention—sure enough, 'Tubthumping' had another surge of popularity—while doing something to placate the Deputy Prime Minister and his supporters. I got on a plane to London and took over as the band's tour manager the following day.

*

Another morally motivated insult was perpetrated by Johnette Napolitano when Concrete Blonde was playing at a benefit gig for the 1994 Northridge earthquake in Los Angeles. The effects of the quake had been felt across the county and a city-wide curfew imposed. I'd flown in from the UK on the first flight allowed in after the curfew was lifted. First class had been full but in economy there were just three people—me and two older ladies who'd been saving for years for their trip to the West Coast and weren't going to let the earthquake stop them. In the circumstances, the whole plane was opened up to everyone. There were passengers lying across rows of seats to sleep.

Shortly after I arrived in LA, I was in the office when a 6.2 magnitude aftershock hit. It was one of the most frightening experiences of my life. We were all badly unsettled and decided to open a bottle of red wine to calm our nerves. Six bottles later, still having to print out the itineraries for the upcoming tour and feeling in no state to look them over, I sent them over to the printers. It was only when we got on the tour that we found the itineraries hadn't printed correctly: the second half of all the telephone numbers for the venues had been chopped off. This was probably my biggest cock-up as a tour manager—though one for which I didn't feel entirely to blame. It wasn't a disaster, but it meant contacting the venues would be much less convenient.

Anyway, while getting ready for the benefit gig, Johnette looked out of the window of her first-floor dressing room and spotted Hugh Hefner's limousine parked below. 'Is he here?' she said. 'What's *he* doing here?' Detesting all that he represented, she looked over the dressing room to see what there was to vandalise his car with. Her eyes alighted on the rider. Out of the window went eggs, sandwiches, spaghetti, melons, langoustine, cold cuts, salad leaves, cheesecake, lemon meringue pie and a bottle of tequila which stripped the expensive paintwork. She shut the window and when asked later in the evening if she had happened to see any vandals outside expressed perfect ignorance of any vandalism having taken place. Once informed of the incident, she suggested that Mr Hefner should perhaps not make his transportation so conspicuous.

Johnette could be rather a handful. I was managing a tour for Concrete Blonde and we were flying from Los Angeles to Australia—a nineteen-hour flight. Plenty of time for Johnette to get bored and it didn't help that she'd been drinking. Having turned up late, we couldn't get the seats we wanted and so we ended up sat right in the middle of the plane. Some of the passengers recognised the band, those who didn't cottoning on that they were personalities of some kind. One guy had kicked up a fuss, lambasting us for swanning up in our sunglasses thinking the world would wait for us. I didn't tell him that we thought nothing of the sort. Over the years, having spent as much time in as many airports as I had, I'd acquired a detailed knowledge of the layout of airports the world over, the length of procedures, the distances from departure lounges to gates. I'd known just how long it would take us to get to the gate, thereby saving us a lot of heel-kicking.

We took off and it wasn't long before Johnette, who hated flying, began seeking diversions. The refreshment trolley came along and provided her with material—ice cubes—which she started throwing at one of the guitar technicians sat in front of her. It wasn't long before projectiles were being hurled the length of the cabin after some of the roadies at the front and back of the plane decided to join in. Johnette threw another ice cube and the piercing shriek of a child filled the cabin. In front of her, a father had been sat with his baby. At that time, children under two years of age could travel free of charge, though they would have to sit on a parent's lap if there was a shortage of seats. The father had been stood up, his baby in his arms, when Johnette threw her ice cube and it had gone down the baby's suit. Incensed, the father called for an attendant, pointed to Johnette and said that she had just thrown an ice cube down his baby's suit. Johnette was by this time completely out of it, having taken sleeping tablets while still being full of booze. A storm of a scene ensued as other passengers offered their two penn'orth, for and against Johnette's behaviour. At one point it looked like the plane was going to be turned round. The attendant, eager to effect a peaceful resolution, asked Johnette to apologise. Johnette wouldn't. The father said she was drunk, how could she ever have been allowed on the plane, she was a threat to his child. Several passengers, evidently Concrete Blonde fans, told him to pipe down, just who did he think he was, it was only a bit of ice. 'It's my *child*!' snapped the man. This went on until, mercifully, the opposing parties tired of their bickering and sat down to endure the rest of the flight—*long* after the poor baby had stopped crying.

Jet-lagged and tired as we were, a day on Bondai beach wasn't perhaps the best idea, but this is what the band wanted. This was in December, the height of summer over there. It was much too hot and several of us started showing symptoms of sun-stroke. We were staying at the Ritz Carlton and by the time we got back there Johnette thought she was coming down with the flu. On the road, most illnesses could be attributed to being run down. Because you had to keep going, however, doctors would be quickly consulted. I had once got rather more than I bargained for—and paid rather more too—when I went to see a Swiss doctor complaining of an aching jaw. He had a look inside my mouth and said that I needed jaw realignment surgery, which would involve the removal of a great many teeth. Having thought I'd just slept on it funny, I said I would see how I felt in a couple of days, thinking I was never going to see *him* again. I was charged £2,000 for the half-hour consultation—and this was in the 1980s.

Anyway, it so happened that also staying at the Ritz Carlton was Madonna. (This is where I'm unclear whether I met her again.) One morning in the lobby I glanced round to see *three* Madonnas walking through. I knew she would be travelling with lookalikes. These were so convincing, however, I'm not sure which, if any, of these three was the real Madonna.

I was to meet her doctor though, of whom there was only one, when he went to see Johnette, who had a steamer installed in her room for her throat. The doctor checked her over and gave her three tablets, one to be taken every six hours. Leaving her room and heading back down the corridor, the doctor said to me that I didn't sound too good myself. I had similar symptoms to Johnette (tight chest, tickling throat, runny nose). Here, he said, and gave me three tablets, the same as he had given Johnette. I took one then and, before getting into bed, asked reception to wake me in six hours' time, when I took the second. By morning, I was healed, my chest, throat, nose, all clear. I'd never known that there was a cure for a cold (cost: $500). But then, when have you ever seen a personality make a public appearance with a cold?

It wasn't long, then, before Johnette was back on form and we went on with the tour. Not having to think of her own health, she was able to think of that of a poor kangaroo we came across by the roadside. We called rescue services, who came out, took the kangaroo to a sanctuary and decided to call it 'CB' for Concrete Blonde, making a nice story for the local press.

I for one was glad to leave Australia. Shortly before Christmas, at another luxurious hotel, I'd had a room on the ground floor, patio doors leading onto the swimming pool. I was on the phone and went to pick up a piece of paper when I strayed too far from the telephone plug and pulled the cord out. Pulling back the bedside table to reconnect, I found a *huge* spider. Bright orange. Though I'm no expert on wildlife, I too this to be a warning to leave well alone. I chucked the phone onto the bed and darted out of the room and went down to the hotel desk to ask someone to see to the removal of my unwelcome guest. The room had to be fumigated before I could go back in and fetch my belongings.

*

It had become a tradition with Concrete Blonde than on the last night of the tour, everyone would dress up. Not just the band, the crew too. And Johnette would choose the costumes. Dressing up wasn't obligatory, though chances were that if you didn't wear your costume, you'd find that you wouldn't be going along on the next tour.

One tour ended at the Greek Theatre in Los Angeles—one of the very best venues where you didn't have to worry about a thing. At their stations, the men found their costumes—long flowing dresses Johnette had picked up at a thrift shop. I was asked by one of the crew if he *really* had to wear his. 'Listen,' I said, 'if you're that good that you're confident you'll be hired for the next tour, don't bother. Otherwise, I'd wear it.' It wasn't so bad for the guys working behind the stage as they would only be seen by the band and crew. It was another matter for the sound and lighting engineers who had to walk through the audience to their desks.

For the internal promotion photos for the 'Bitches on Wheels' tour (the 'bitches' being Johnette, Holly Vincent, from the support act, and myself), all the band had been wearing chicken heads. The last night of the tour, then, everyone had to dress up as chickens, which meant applying red stage make-up to faces, arms and legs. (For those of us backstage, thankfully, we were able to get away with just daubing our faces and hands.) Johnette, however, most of whose arms and legs were exposed, was covered in the stuff. After the gig, we went to wash off our make-up. Johnette, however, had had a few drinks and had fallen asleep before removing her costume. She couldn't be woken up, and so, having an early flight to catch, we bundled her onto the tour bus and had to carry her through the airport. While we dug out our tickets, we laid her in front of the check-in desk covered in her hardened stage make-up with her chicken head on.

*

Outrageous as the behaviour of some artists can be, rarely, if ever, do they allow it to get in the way of their work. Occasionally, though, it does. Concrete Blonde were playing in Phoenix and during the sound checks we discovered that the drummer was missing. The checks were done in his absence and I went to find him. I combed the venue and found that he had disappeared. He could have been anywhere in Phoenix and I didn't have any way of getting in touch with him. So, when the doors opened, I waited outside the venue intending to ask those on the guest-list who mentioned the drummer's name if they knew where he was. One of his friends told me the last time she had seen him he had been with friends, smoking dope on a mountainside. *Great*, I thought.

At last he showed up, in the nick of time, though it wasn't any good that he did: he was so high he could barely speak. I practically poured five huge pots of coffee down his throat and gave him two Redoxon tables. (Tour managers always used to have these to hand in case of someone's being loaded or high—to give them a boost, make them be sick, work a placebo effect.) All this wasn't sufficient to bring him round, though. The band played a great acoustic set and no one remarked on the drummerlessness.

On another tour, the same thing happened again. We were ready to make the sound checks and he'd gone. I think he must have felt quite isolated; feelings weren't great between him and the rest of the band. Thinking that he must be on the tour bus, I went to look. I checked all the bunks but couldn't find him. The one place I didn't look was the driver's bunk, there being an unwritten law that one didn't encroach on the driver's cabin. I think he must have been there, though I couldn't say for sure. I never saw him again. One of the roadies stood in for him for a week-and-a-half before a new drummer was enlisted to join the tour.

I knew another artist for whom drugs also got in the way of his work. He was young when he got his break. Being from a family who didn't have a lot of money, he suddenly found himself with money in excess. One day we were booked in at a rehearsal studio in Birmingham and he was late. I called him to see where he was. He said he was at a garage, his car was broken. 'Broken?' I said. 'You've only had it a few days.' He told me not to worry, he was buying a new one. I asked if I'd heard him right. I had. He told me his car had wrapped around a traffic light. I asked him where it was. Wrapped round the traffic light, he told me. He said he would see me shortly. 'Hold on,' I said. 'You can't crash your car and then just go and get another one.' Sure he could, he told me, he had plenty of money. I said I knew he had a lot of money. I asked him which garage he was at and told him I would be there as soon as I could and not to buy a car before I got there. I left the studio and got to the garage just as he was about to sign on the dotted line for an identical brand new car.

It was an unfortunate thing to have made it so young. He had been awarded NME's Newcomer of the Year Award. All that money, all that temptation. It wasn't long before he was hooked on dope. It got so bad that he started hallucinating, seeing things jump out of the television. He hadn't slept for a fortnight and wouldn't go to the door. He was admitted to a Priory hospital for rehabilitation. In the end, he couldn't work anymore—not doing what he had been. He simply couldn't function. It was so sad, one of the most tragic situations I've ever been involved in.

*

In some cases, badness is in the eye of the beholder. For a time I worked as tour manager for Credit to the Nation. Fronted by Matty Hanson, they were one of the first rap acts in the UK and had done very well for themselves, touring with the Levellers and Chumbawamba. With the latter they had made the single 'Enough is Enough'. After their hits 'Call It What You Want' and 'Teenage

Sensation' (which is what Matty was), they started getting more radio plays than Chumbawamba and the relative standing of the bands flipped, until Chumbawamba released 'Tubthumping' in 1997. Credit to the Nation also toured with Manic Street Preachers on their 1993 'Gold Against the Soul' tour. Guitarist Richey Edwards was with the band then. I remember being shocked to hear of his disappearance not that long after.

Matty and the guys came from good families but they had not had a privileged upbringing. We were away for a few days and were to stay the first night at a hotel in Harrogate. It was a country house hotel, expensive and traditional. The guys hadn't stayed in a hotel before. They were dressed in jeans and trainers. One of them, a dancer, had his things in a carrier bag. There were porters at the door and a bell-boy came forward to take the luggage. 'Oi!' shouted one of the guys. 'What d'you think you're doing? Get your hands off my bag!' I said it was alright, the bell-boy explaining he was taking his bag up to his room for him. The guests sat out on the verandah taking tea observed the scene with interest.

Another time it was the hotel that caused the embarrassme The guys were playing a gig in Anglesey, in North Wales. We the hotel we were staying at, one of the few that had rooms available at that time of the year (the height of summer), and which was popular with showbusiness people. We walked through the lobby and I saw the guy's expressions turn sour. I looked around to see what was amiss. At first I couldn't see it. Then I did. On the walls were pictures of the Black and White Minstrels. It turned out that the proprietor of the hotel had been one of the Minstrels and was evidently quite proud of the fact, proud enough to have all these pictures up anyway. At first the guys were really quite put out about it—and understandably. The proprietor was obviously very embarrassed and after an awkward conversation, the guys realised he wasn't a frothing racist and they let it go. I'm sure nowadays he wouldn't have been allowed to hang those pictures, and if he had, I doubt he'd have wanted to.

*

the ones at the centre of things, it isn't just the

mbers of the crew can behave just as

excellent opportunities for smuggling—not

got to

just drugs, guns too. Because of the tight schedules and the amount of equipment that goes on tour with them, customs officials often allow bands to pass through checks without making complete inspections of their luggage. Often, an official will make a partial random inspection, asking to look inside a particular case—29, say. Case 29 will be brought out (hopefully it isn't at the front of the hold, otherwise all the other cases will have to be removed to get to it) and its contents checked against those stated. If the actual and stated contents match up, the lot will be allowed through. A discrepancy will result in a more thorough inspection. The opportunity that this creates for smuggling has not gone unexploited.

Bad as all this may be, the scale of these operations is pretty small. It was in Miami with Concrete Blonde that I got a sense of just how large operations can be and how well crime can pay. The venue they were playing was palatial, one of the most opulent I've ever come across. We arrived in the daytime, when venues usually look their worst because then you can actually see them. (Once you have seen some of these places in the daytime, you think carefully about dressing up and never put on your best.) This venue, however, in broad shining daylight looked magnificent. We got backstage, where things are normally even worse (in one dressing room, a mouse popped up beside me from the back of a sofa), and found it just as luxurious as the rest of the place. There were offices for the manager and the production manager. You could almost hear the groaning of the catering tables, well in excess of the rider. It occurred to me that this was much too nice a place for an alternative rock band to play. (That is no insult to alternative rock bands, by the way.)

I was on my way backstage when I noticed one of the merchandisers looking rather perturbed. I asked him if he was alright. He said not really, no. I asked him what was wrong. He pointed to a light switch. 'Turn that.' 'Turn it?' I said. 'How? It's a flick-switch.' He told me to turn the whole unit, showing me with his hand. I did so and the wall slowly slid backwards. I knew this shouldn't be happening, as we weren't in a movie. Nevertheless, there before us was an exquisitely furnished cavern—crystal chandeliers, wide spiralling staircases, broad-shouldered men in beautifully tailored suits, gorgeous women in shimmering dresses. It all said one thing to me: drugs. It was then that I realised that the place *was* too nice for an alternative rock band and that the real reason we were there was to help with the laundry. I suggested to the merchandiser that we leave them to it and get ready for the show.

When it came to it, my earlier suspicions were confirmed. The audience weren't really watching the show. I had a sense of evil, of malignant machinery hidden behind all the glitz and glamour, which we, the band and crew, were helping turn. I looked forward to getting out of there, but didn't expect that it would be quite so soon.

Another piece of expensive equipment the venue had was a state-of-the-art lighting desk. Johnette hated moving lights and prohibited their use during shows. The temptation too great, however, on one of the songs the lighting technician started playing with the moving lights. Halfway through, Johnette stopped. One of the other things which had been provided in excess of the rider was a bottle of very good, very expensive tequila. Earlier in the day she had fallen out with everybody over everything and the tequila hadn't helped any. She had gone to a hairdressers that afternoon and dyed her hair electric blue. When she came offstage she gave me the most evil of eyes.

She left the venue and I went after her. I had to go and finalise the bill at the hotel and wanted to make sure she got back alright. When I entered the lobby she was at the front desk and asked me what I was doing there, said I should be overseeing the packing-up of the equipment (something I never did). I went outside and waited for her to go up to her room before going back in to get the receipts. We picked her up in the bus later on, as we had to drive overnight to the next venue. She was in the foulest mood, effing and blinding, and couldn't be calmed down. As she passed my bunk, she kicked out, missed me, and fell over. I decided that was it. The tour had gone on a week longer than it should have, I'd had enough, I wanted to go home. We got to the hotel at 4 am. I called management and told them that if I didn't receive an apology from Johnette, that was it, I was leaving, I'd catch a flight out of Orlando. Later that afternoon, at 4 pm, I got an apology from Johnette, and we finished the tour.

*

Given how alcohol can disrupt the work, it's surprising the role it plays in creating it. Many an idea for an act or an album has come up from a martini or a glass of red—usually several martinis and several glasses of red. The idea for the Smurfs doing covers of pop songs slipped out of the drunken haze of two A&R guys from EMI. Another such idea was that had by the guitarist Paul Guerin and an EMI executive over a drink one night in Belfast. Performing at the club that night was an Elvis Presley impersonator who was very good, the best they'd ever seen. They had the idea of getting him to do an album of non-Elvis songs and started putting together a track-list. As the list grew, they realised that all the songs they had suggested were done by artists who had died. This was the revelation which led to the idea for *Gravelands*—an album of covers of non-Elvis songs by deceased artists sung as Elvis would have sung them.

When the set was finished they made their way backstage to meet him. His name was James Brown, born in Belfast. He was a postman and did his Elvis acts on the side. The EMI man asked him how he'd like to make a record and told him about the idea for *Gravelands*. James didn't look so sure. The EMI man told him he was the best Elvis impersonator he'd seen and that he believed he could make a lot of money. This gave him pause. He was Irish Catholic and had a lot of children, having been married very young. If he signed with EMI, he could move out of his small flat above an off-licence and buy his own house with central heating. He signed, got his advance and made the record, which was a hit, and went on to sell half-a-million copies. From the album's conception to release, all had gone smoothly. It was only then that a bump was hit—and it was a big one: James said he wouldn't go on tour.

This was a shock. Until that point, everyone had assumed that he would be up for it. He flatly refused, however. He was told that he *had* to go on tour to sell his records. In the end, he was persuaded to go on the road and for a time it looked like all would be well. No one had foreseen what a lot of bumps still lay ahead.

It reached a point where we would be waiting at the airport and he wouldn't show up. This was often due to his wife, a hot-tempered woman with jet black hair and jade green eyes, who hated his performing on account of the attention it brought him from other women. He wouldn't travel on the tour bus and made his own way to the venues. He insisted that his family come along with him—not just his wife and children, but his aunts and uncles and cousins.

He could definitely draw an audience, both sides of the Atlantic. Jim was one of the acts at SXSW and Robbie Williams turned up at the bar where he was performing wearing a huge straw stetson. In England he had heard Jim's *Gravelands* and wanted to meet him. Right Said Fred had been on before. It was rather surreal hearing 'I'm Too Sexy' followed by Kurt Cobain's 'I'm Yours' as sung by Elvis.

When we met Robbie after the gig he invited us to go and watch his show at one of the open-air venues. We had to run from the venue Jim had been playing. Unbeknownst to me, Robbie had a documentary film crew with him. The cameras were pointed down the street as we ran. I've never seen the footage and I hope it no longer exists.

After Robbie's show we went to the DoubleTree hotel, where he was staying, to discuss the possibility of a collaboration between him and Jim. At the time Robbie was trying to break America. As an Elvis impersonator, widely regarded as the best around, and being called James Brown, Jim had gone down *very* well with the Americans. Robbie had his own suite at the hotel but it was almost entirely bereft of furniture, hence I ended up sitting on his bed. There *had* been furniture in the suite but he had asked for it to be removed so he could convert the lounge into a football pitch, two sets of goalposts put up at either end. I sat on his bed for two hours, looking through the bedroom's double doorway, watching Robbie doing keepie-uppies and practising his penalty shots while we talked about his duetting with Jim. (I should perhaps add that this was all I did on Robbie's bed.)

In Germany he had a string of television appearances. The Coors were also performing on these shows so we'd always be bumping into each other at the studios. One quite bizarre gig James had was a private party for a friend of the presenter and DJ Chris Evans, which Chris had helped to organise.

There was a big gig in Cologne and as he was preparing to go onstage he had a massive row with his wife. He took off his costume and refused to perform. I sat down with them both, calmed them down, reassured his wife that she was not in any danger of losing her husband to his lustful fans and persuaded him to get out there. Before going in to speak with them, I had gone to the toilets to remove my make-up and dress myself down a bit so as not to intimidate or provoke his wife. He agreed to perform and went to get dressed, meanwhile excuses were made for his lateness.

At the sides of the stage cannons were set to fire confetti over the audience as he walked out. He was stood in the wings, at last ready to go out, when his wife noticed in the front row of the audience a big-bosomed woman making a pendulous display for her husband. As he stepped out onto the stage, the cannons firing, with the confetti shot into the air, up went a wedding ring. His wife shrieked and stormed off, meanwhile the music burst from the speakers, the confetti showering the audience and I went down on my hands and knees, scrabbling for the ring. I found it, thank God, and kept it firmly in my palm for the rest of the show.

As he received his final applause, the King came off the stage and went back to his dressing room where the German promoter had generously brought out a large cake to celebrate his success. His wife was livid and started hurling cake around the room along with her accusations. The promoter thought to deprive her of her ammunition and removed the cake to his car. Jim's manager, who had flown out for the occasion, noticing my lack of make-up, said that he hadn't ever seen me without any. I explained to him what had gone on earlier and that if I hadn't, there almost certainly wouldn't have been any show.

It was part of James's contract with EMI that he would make a second album. A studio was hired in Spain and a villa was rented nearby in which he could stay with his family. I was to stay in the villa too so that I could keep an eye on him, make sure he was alright and that he turned up at the studio. I took Kennedy, my daughter, along with me, and we shared a large bedroom with an en-suite which meant we were able to keep out of the way of the family. When I got back to the villa after the first day at the studio, I found the place overrun with children. I went to my room and a man I had never seen before walked out and told me he had just put his toiletries in the bathroom. I asked the man who he was and he told me was a cousin of James's. It turned out that the people in the house were James's family who had all got cheap flights from Ireland having accepted his invitation to holiday at the villa while he worked on the album. I put my foot down and declared mine and Kennedy's room out of bounds. There were people everywhere, sleeping on sofas, inflated lilos, in bathtubs.

I had been on tour with another band before going on the next one with James. I landed in Heathrow, in time for the flight to Los Angeles. I kept looking at my watch as we waited for James. Eventually I realised he wasn't going to show up. I got on the phone. It turned out he was still at home—in Belfast. He said he wouldn't go on tour unless his uncle could come too. What was so funny (less so at the time) was that he got so uptight about all the immediate luxuries that going on tour with a major label afforded and hated last-minute changes, yet he was constantly taking advantage of the former and making the latter. In addition to his absurdly jealous wife, the problem was that he simply didn't want to be famous. What he wanted was a better life for his family. Materially, things had improved a lot, and the last I heard from James he was living happily in his hometown of Belfast, his children grown up and still with the love of his life.

11

Bringing Up Baby

Katharine Hepburn said that women couldn't have it all—
children and a career. Never having wanted children, I didn't mean
to try, only things turned out otherwise. I found that women *can*
have both, though whether they should is another matter, a question
of what, and who, matters most.

*

I was on tour with Hawkwind, who were playing Freetown
Christiania, the hippy commune established in a disused military
base in Copenhagen. (This was one place you were assured of the
restaurants catering for vegetarians.) I wasn't feeling well. I hadn't
been feeling great for a few days but it was when we got to
Christiania that I began to feel really sick. Terrible nausea. I thought
it must have been the aloo gobi I'd had the night before, the thought
of which made my stomach turn, as did almost all other food save

MacDonald's vanilla milkshake, for which I felt a sudden, fierce craving. I went on with the tour, the nausea coming and going, feeling more than usually tired. By Christmas I was feeling really fatigued. Putting it down to a vitamin deficiency, I decided that I'd see about getting a B12 boost after Christmas and booked myself in for a consultation. I went along, told the doctor my symptoms and was taken aback when he asked me if it had occurred to me that I might be pregnant.

'Pregnant?' I blurted. 'I'm not *pregnant.*'

I said I thought it was a B12 deficiency; a boost would sort me out. He said he'd like me to take a pregnancy test. I was certain I couldn't be pregnant. Almost certain. The last time I'd seen my second husband was a week in September. It had been with regret that I'd calculated that, with us both working on separate tours, we'd seen each for just three weeks that year. I took the test and it came back positive. There was a small chance of its being a false positive, but it was a small one. So, I thought… I'm pregnant.

As I said, I hadn't wanted a child. Now I had a baby well on its way. It was going to be an eventful year. Once the festivities were over, I went back to work. An assistant accompanied me the last few weeks I was expecting, doing any running around for me. I kept up a pace, though, mindful of the baby, I was careful not to strain myself. I was particularly anxious about all the noise, keeping away from the speakers during sound checks. I wondered whether it would have any influence on the baby's musical tastes. For a long time, I hadn't shown, then suddenly I had. I'd had to take off my jeans to go in for an appointment with the doctor. Thankfully, I was wearing a long jumper.

I worked right up until the week before I gave birth. I finished on a Saturday, got home on the Sunday and the following Sunday I went into hospital. It was a difficult labour lasting forty-eight hours. The baby—a girl, Kennedy—was thankfully okay. It was quite something to meet her. The ordeal of delivery overcome, I decided to make the most of my hospital stay. It was just as well that I did since the moment I stepped out of the hospital my phone rang. It was the office: an American tour, how soon could I leave.

'I've just had a baby,' I said. 'I'm in the hospital car park.'

'Oh right. Well. How soon can you leave?'

I said I was sorry, I couldn't do it. Couldn't possibly. In the end, I went over and joined the tour for the last two weeks. I hated it.

I couldn't bear being away from Kennedy. I could have carried on, but I didn't want to. I went to the office and explained the reason for my resignation. I was offered a promotion—a great job, the promise of work for decades. I turned it down. Sweeteners were added—money, perks. No, I said. I was sorry, I just didn't want it.

And so my days as a tour manager were over. It was sad but I knew it was the right decision. I had a sound engineer friend who'd told me how she might not see her son for six months at a stretch. Those two weeks away from Kennedy had been too long. I didn't stop working though. It wasn't long before I started working as a troubleshooter. If there was a problem with a tour, I'd be sent out to solve it. While this meant I was often going away, the stints weren't long, nothing like what it would be if I was still tour-managing. My mum was amazing, looking after Kennedy when I went away. Sometimes Kennedy would come with me. I used to take her onstage. She had been to California several times before she was two. The only nuisance was having her on my knee during the flight.

I remember taking her to see S Club 7. (This was something I'd thought we'd do a lot together—going to gigs.) We were sat in the gods and had a steep climb up a set of concrete steps—without railings, in the dark, lights flashing around us, laden with popcorn and drinks. I'm not an habitual complainer but I got a bit arsey and went to complain to a steward, pointing out how easy it would be to have an accident climbing up those steps, and how dangerous one would be. With a little help from my name and reputation, we were given tickets right next to the stage. I thought Kennedy would be thrilled. After the show, however, she asked me never to take her to another gig again. It wasn't the embarrassment of my having complained, it was the fact that I'd spoiled all the surprises, knowing just what was what onstage and off. As we'd been making our way to our seats, Kennedy, hurrying, had said, 'Quick; it's going to start in ten minutes.' I explained that it wouldn't be starting for another half-hour; there was this and this still to do. Before the performance, someone came onstage to apologise for a slight delay, giving an explanation that was obviously (to me) a lot of nonsense. Seeing how the stage was set, I said there would be people coming on from there and there, pointing to the wings, while S Club would be coming up through the floor. 'And look at that,' I said, pointing over our heads. 'They're going to walk out over the audience.' I should have known better. As it was, it was only afterwards that I realised what a disappoint it must have been.

A few years later, when Kennedy was in her teens, I was able to do something to make up for it. Her favourite band was My Chemical Romance and I was able to get her VIP tickets to go and see them. They didn't have to queue, their seats were in an exclusive roped-off area and they were sat next to a TV soap opera star. I didn't often try to work things like this but I was very glad to have been able to work this one.

*

When we first went out to America—my mum, Kennedy and me—I really had only one desideratum regarding where we lived: that we be near an airport. I'd thought we might settle in Florida, so that's where we went. We stayed there five days. Since I was no longer working with a band, being English, we were treated like tourists. The place was teeming with them. You had no trouble picking them out: either pasty or sunburnt (never in-between), no shirts, Union Jack swimming shorts, quaffing lager. There was no way we'd be settling in Florida. So we loaded up the people carrier and set off, me and my mum in the front, the cat and the dog behind, Kennedy with her toys behind them, our luggage piled up in the boot. We were like the Beverly Hillbillies. We got on the I-10 and headed west, looking out of the windows to see where we might call home.

I knew that we'd stop before reaching California. I didn't want Kennedy to go to school there. A friend of mine had a son who'd gone to Torrance High School (as featured in *Beverly Hills, 90210*) and he'd had a rough time there. Though he didn't want for anything, he wasn't spoilt as many of his classmates were—he didn't have a Porsche to drive to school in or a three million-dollar tree-house, and he'd found himself isolated because of it. He wasn't a bad kid but he had got in with a bad crowd. It wasn't just the other kids who discriminated against him: one night the police stopped him while he was riding home on his bike—not driving a car and not as well-dressed as many of the other kids in the area. I didn't want to risk the same thing happening to Kennedy.

We'd been driving for days when we got to Phoenix. Not much further and we'd be in LA. I asked mum and Kennedy what they thought of the place. It was conveniently near LA, the flight to LAX taking just forty-five minutes. Breathtaking landscapes, fabulous weather. We decided we could call this home, and soon we did.

At this time I wasn't working as a troubleshooter anymore having gone back to tour-managing, though really I was a step above, working only short tours, usually one-week stints. I gave this up, however, when my mum became unwell so that I could take care of her. It was the turnaround of generations, the familial circle: my mum had looked after me; now I was going to look after her.

Living where we were, though, other things started to intrude. Because of the connections that had been made and the trust built up while working with a number of people in the LA music scene and now living so near, when I was asked if I wanted to help with a project, I found it difficult to say no. These were good friends—almost all the people I worked with became good friends— and I didn't want to disappoint them, but I'd withdrawn from that world. It was only once I'd left that I fully realised how dependent some of them had been on me for handling the world of everyday. For some of them, for years I had been telling them when they would be getting up, where they would be going, how they were to get there. So I'd find myself being asked what to do about faulty plumbing and broken washing machines. In England, there hadn't been any possibility of my knowing any Angeleno plumbers and repairmen to recommend. Now, just across the state border, it seemed I might be able to help.

As a little aside, nearness is a relative matter. In England, a friend who lives an hour's drive away doesn't live near you. In America, a friend who lives a three-hour drive away does. My American friends would think nothing of driving two or three hours to go out for dinner. In fairness, the roads over there aren't like British roads. I remember one time I was driving down an interstate and saw a sign saying roadworks for 94 miles. If I'd seen this going down the M6 I would have started to feel quite ill. As it was, another temporary road had been thrown up alongside the interstate; I never even noticed the roadworks. Even still, this was one aspect of American life I never got used to.

It wasn't all bad being near LA. I remember going to Johnette Napolitano's bungalow in the Hollywood hills and taking Kennedy with me. In the dining room Johnette had a magnificent dining table, about eighteen feet long, gleaming mahogany, the chairs beautifully turned and upholstered. I had some work to do so I left Kennedy with Johnette and Richard, her childminder. 'You don't mind me leaving her with you?' I said to Johnette. 'Oh no,' she replied. 'We've got some clay to make pots.' When I got back I was surprised to see that it was real clay that Johnette had been talking about, great clumps of the stuff, from which they'd hacked pieces to shape into pots. What most took me aback, however, was where they'd been doing it. The dining table was smeared with clay, scored with knifemarks, Kennedy kneeling up on one of the chairs, her hands filthy. I couldn't believe it. That magnificent table must have been ruined.

Unkind as it might sound, some of those you became friends with for a season in your life you don't wish to remain friends with forever. This was something I found living in the States. Part of it has to do with the fact that when you're working as a tour manager, you're dealing with other people's problems and people don't necessarily appreciate, or even seem to entertain the possibility, that you have problems of your own. In the role, you're responsible for people, looking out for them, making sure they get what they need.

The relationship therefore ends up being rather one-way. For all the years you've known them, you've been taking a keen interest in them while they might not have all that much of an interest in you.

I myself, however, had received a lot of support when I'd been in the industry, and I realised just how much only once I'd left it. As a tour manager, I'd become used to immediacy: things that needed to get done got done straightaway—waiting around wasn't an option. A *week* to wait for the plumber to come out and service my boiler? That seemed a lifetime away. I found that I had to deal with obstacles I hadn't even noticed before—at least, not for a very long time. I'd always had a team behind me working to ensure that anything I couldn't sort out myself would be sorted for me. Without that backup, I had to deal with things myself—and wait however long that took. It was a shock how normal life takes forever.

There was no chance of my going back, though, not with the responsibility I had for my family—the most important thing in my life. One chapter had finished and another had begun.

12

Unlucky for Some (In Love)

Or: SEX & Drugs & Rock & Roll

This is a story beginning in the 1970s, when everyone was brought up with Ian Dury and 'Sex & Drugs & Rock & Roll'. So far we've had lots of rock 'n' roll and a fair amount of drugs. Now I guess it's time for sex (or not, as the case may be).

The big questions, I suppose will be: Did I? And who with?

Though I hate to disappoint, the answer to the first, which cancels the second, is No. That's not to say I wasn't aware of all sorts going on around me, nor that I didn't even see things. Some of the groupies I encountered throughout my career were some of the most stunning women I've ever seen. Many of them have written their own accounts of what went on backstage.

The relationships I had with the bands I worked with were both professional and personal. The personal aspect, however, was one of friendship. Bands often used to refer to their wives/girlfriends/groupies/females of any sort (not very flatteringly) as 'boilers' and would designate certain tours as 'No boiler tours'. I therefore found that on a number of tours I was the only woman around but treated as one of them. This was something I enjoyed. It was nice to have the affection of these (often charismatic) guys uncomplicated by sex. As a merchandise seller, young and inexperienced, travelling through strange far-flung towns, these friendships gave me a security for which I was extremely grateful. I was a friend to the guys and they were a friend to me. That was how it was. Simple. Until, that is, I met my first husband in 1980 and got married (I feel) far too young three years later.

The marriage didn't last. Partly, I think, this was due to the pressure of my touring. By the time we were married, Michael had given it up. He had started touring in the first place more as a favour to his uncle, Geezer Butler, than anything else, and the favour had led to a permanent job. He'd done it long enough to know, however, that a lot of affection would be shown to me, as I knew the affection of women would be shown to him. Jealousy was therefore a major part of our relationship from the start.

Nor were his worries unfounded, as I came to be involved with my second husband, an affair which led to the break up of our marriage. Sadly, this marriage didn't last either. As you can imagine, the amount of drugs and alcohol that were around, addiction can take hold of a person and change them. It also didn't help that, when I was tour-managing, I had the top job. My earning a salary twice as large as my husband's didn't add to his self-esteem.

That's really all I have to say on this subject. Although this chapter may be a bit of a disappointment, in that respect it's rather like my love-life.

13

Living the Dream

I started out selling T-shirts and ended up as a tour manager for some of the most biggest bands in rock 'n' roll history. I made it. I reached the top. At least as far as touring was concerned, there wasn't any higher I could climb. Yet I felt—not necessarily at the time, but increasingly with the passing of the years—that the best job I'd had was my first. I heard that Nick Alexander, a merchandise seller for Eagles of Death Metal, one of those tragically killed in the Bataclan terrorist attacks of 2015, was to have said to his girlfriend how much he loved his job and considered it the best in the world. When I heard this, I knew just what he meant. Being a merchandiser *was* the best job in the world.

While I didn't have the power and prestige I had as a tour manager, I also didn't have all the responsibility which was often so oppressive and alienating. It wasn't nearly as much of a laugh and the pressures applied from all directions could bring you to tears (behind closed doors). There was a time when the thing I most looked forward to was sleep—that period of sweet unconsciousness when I didn't have to think about everything I had to do. This is one forewarning I would give to anyone considering a career in tour-management. It's consuming.

When I went into tour-management there were no university courses on the subject. Some years ago I was asked to feature in a book on unusual job descriptions. I wouldn't receive such an invitation now. Along with the courses in music production and music management, you can take a course on tour-management. Taking a course isn't enough, however. Experience is essential. I became a tour manager (with Motörhead) because I'd been working with bands for years and I knew Motörhead first-hand—how they liked to work, how they performed, what went into a show, how their tours were organised and who was responsible for what. As my employers knew, there was nothing any band could do that would come close to matching Motörhead's antics, so I guess you could I say I'd seen it all. Having toured with other bands, I knew what they did in common with other bands and what liked to do their own way. All this I knew from years selling T-shirts. I was initially asked to take on the responsibility for one night only because I'd demonstrated my capacities. I had the trust of my employers who'd seen what I'd done and knew what I was capable of—even if I didn't know it myself at the time. It was that one night that set me on the path to becoming a tour manager.

I would therefore say to anyone aspiring to the vocation, don't expect that you can do a course and then go and work for a band if you haven't worked with them before. A tour manager needs to know about everyone else's role, from the rigger's to the bus driver's, so they can see that everything gets done that needs to get done. A good show depends on everybody making their contribution. Absolutely crucial is the anticipation of problems so you can make sure they don't arise. For one rather outlandish example, when I was touring with Chumbawamba we were staying at the magnificent Soho Grand Hotel in New York. In every room there was a goldfish. Knowing how quickly things could get out hand, I made sure that every goldfish bowl was removed beforehand.

There's no leaving anything till tomorrow. There isn't a tomorrow. The show has to play and there are no second chances. This kind of practical knowledge can only be acquired through experience. Nowadays, with such high degrees of specialisation, when acts travel with their own dentists, doctors, makeup artists, stylists, minders—you name it, they have *at least* one of them—there's even more to keep track of.

When problems do arise, you have to know who to go to—if you can't fix them yourself, that is. Also important is knowing who *not* to go to: the only people who should know about a problem are those who can do something about it. You have to be blunt and direct—there's no time for sugar-coating and sparing feelings. One time I had to tell two crew members—a sound engineer and a lighting engineer—that they weren't coming with us to Australia. I decided to tell them before rather than after that night's show so that if they were going to get uptight about it, they'd do so before they'd had a few post-show drinks. If they threw a hissy fit, I had two other engineers on standby who could be drafted in to replace them.

You're always working with people, and people aren't always predictable. You'll no doubt have your problems too. But don't expect others to listen to them. Most likely you'll be listening to theirs. (Credit to the Nation made me a badge saying 'Kim'll Fix It'. Though the associations with this little joke are no longer happy, it says something about the expectations bands have that a tour manager is there to solve their problems.) As a tour manager, you'll need a certain amount of inner strength.

Like all managers, a tour manager has to bring the best out of their team. This requires taking an interest and concern in each person, knowing when someone needs an encouraging word, when they need a kick in the pants and when they just need leaving alone. It involves letting people know that you appreciate them. One time, we found upon arrival that some of the equipment was damaged. This meant one of the roadies having to spend his evening fixing it while everyone else was sipping cocktails and watching the sun go down. How do you make it up to someone when they do something like that? You get them a favourite bottle, you give them a good lunch. Small tokens, maybe, but tokens nevertheless of your appreciation. When I was with a band at SXSW one time and they were asked to perform last-minute, this meant everyone losing their free evening. The next night I took them all out to dinner. This might sound patronising or manipulative but it isn't. It's just common decency: when another person has done above and beyond their duty, you should show gratitude. When someone simply does their duty, it's nice to do the same.

All those years travelling with bands selling T-shirts I was building up knowledge of a great many places the world over—of roads, airports, hotels, cafés, restaurants, high streets, car hire centres—all of which I put to use in my time managing tours. You arrive in a new town late at night. Where do you get some dry cleaning done? Where can you get a decent meal at that time? And does it cater for vegans? These are the kind of things you should know and they're the kinds of things you can know only by travelling—perhaps only by travelling as a tour travels—needing to find places to eat and drink and get your clothes dry-cleaned at the craziest of hours. Yes, there's Google, but there's nothing like the personal touch. In addition to knowing where to shop, more importantly, you know what to shop for—Chanel in Paris, knock-offs in New York. Plus, when you've been around, people get to know who you are. There's nothing like checking in to British Airways Economy and the staff knowing you while those around are left wondering.

All the experience by which you acquire this knowledge can't be got through shadowing. If someone had asked to shadow me when I was working as a tour manager, I'd have said no.

Straightaway. I can't imagine any tour manager in their right mind saying yes. For one thing, who's to say you wouldn't be party to some outrageousness, large or small, and want to talk about it later. No thank you. Joining a tour is almost certainly the best thing you can do, and since, if you're just starting out, there won't be any chance of you doing so as a tour manager, you should do so in some other, lesser role.

Remember, though, that lesser doesn't mean less fun. As I said, selling T-shirts was the best job I ever had. Chances are, tour-management isn't as glamorous as you think it is. That's not to say it can't be very glamorous, though if it's fame you seek as well as riches, I'd suggest you take another path. If, however, you want to live like a rock star and you're not bothered about being famous (personally, I can't think of anything worse), it's quite possibly for you.

What I would give, then, as the single most important piece of advice is to try and get a job working with a band in whatever capacity you can. Alternatively, try getting work at a concert venue. Do anything: sell programmes, work in the café, push boxes, pack trucks. Get to know what goes into putting on a show, get to know the people who work the venue, who puts on the shows, who goes out onstage. Ask questions, look to learn, make contacts. Show that you're keen and take whatever opportunities you can to show what you can do—and hopefully, what you're capable of doing.

Though times have changed since when I started out, there's no question it's harder to become a tour manager if you're a woman. It shouldn't be, but it is. Some guys—and as a tour manager you're often working with guys—just don't like a woman telling them what to do. That creates an extra pressure to perform, to make sure that you don't slip up. There were times I definitely felt this.

In saying that, however, there were occasions when I turned my femininity to my advantage. (In America, the British accent helped too.) One time the promoter had arranged a buy-out for the band and the only place open at that time of night was a pizzeria. I must have rolled my eyes: it would have been pizza for the third night in a row. 'Didn't we like pizza?' the promoter asked. I explained that we were pizzaed out. He told me that he knew a place that did the most delicious hot roast beef sandwiches and mashed potato, only it was some distance away. Nevertheless, he said if we wanted to order food from there he would go and collect it for us. He called the restaurant and asked what they had on the menu that night. We all placed an order and he went to pick it up. I may have fluttered my eyelashes a little, but that was all. If I'd been a man, it would almost certainly have been pizza.

Isn't this just as bad, though—just another form of sexism? I don't think so. Did I mind not having pizza again because I was a woman? Not a bit. Do I mind a man holding a door open for me? I'd mind more if he didn't. The real danger, as I see it, is taking things too seriously. Of course there are boundaries—unwanted advances, degrading conduct, plain abuse. But there are many intersexual interactions that don't do any harm and which can be a leavening source of pleasure and fun. If you don't like them, just ignore them.

Being a tour manager is tough. You're only as good as your last ten minutes. That being said, don't think, if you are a woman, that that means you have to do the job like a man. Whatever my name might have suggested to the contrary, I wore designer shoes instead of steel toe-caps, freshly-painted nail varnish instead of tattoos and carried a Tiffany pen instead of a spanner in my back pocket. I had no interest in being one of the guys, let alone proving it. I've known girls to lug flight cases about when they really shouldn't have been. And I don't just mean for physical reasons: I mean it wasn't their job to do it—there were guys who were paid to do such lugging. I don't mean to say that, as a tour manager, a woman *can't* do these things, only that she doesn't need to. Don't think for a moment you need to be a man. You don't. Be whoever you want to be.

That's what I did.

Afterword

A group of students taking a tour-management course were told that a tour manager called Kim was coming to speak to them. They were asked to write down what they expected Kim to be like. Here are some of their answers:

A bald shaven-headed man. - Neil

A very very butch female. - Leanne

A skin-head type. - Paul

A guy with thick heavy boots, rough, with a lot of tattoos—on his head, his arms. - Jess

A little short fat man. - Callum

As you'll have seen from the photos, there are exceptions to these generalisations.

Special Thanks

Doreen Hawes – *The best mum*

Kennedy Stewart-Hawes – *An amazing daughter*

Lemmy Kilmister & Motorhead – *The best teachers*

Doug Smith & Eve Carr – *Giving a 19 year-old girl the opportunity of an exceptional life*

Viv Larimer – *Without whom the book would not be possible*

Josh Lawford

Jo Hilditch & Ash Kiely

And

All the bands and crew from here to America

Made in the USA
Middletown, DE
25 March 2021